A Guy's Guide to Style

Acknowledgements

I thank my wife Bettina for her support, Erill Fritz for his patience, and all the staff at h.f.ullmann for their kindness in spite of time pressure in the final stages.

I thank all those who have made pictures available without charge, especially the companies Belvest, Cove & Co., Eduard Meier, Scabal, and Timberland. My special thanks go to Schuh Konzept in Berlin for their generous loan of shoes.

© h.f.ullmann publishing GmbH
Original title: *Mode Guide für Männer*
Original ISBN: 978-3-8480-0027-2

Project management: Lars Pietzschmann
Photos: erill.fritz.fotografien.
Design and typesetting: e.fritz, berlin06
Production department: Sabine Vogt

Cover photo: © mauritius images / age

© for the English edition: h.f.ullmann publishing GmbH

Translation from German by Susan Ghanouni
in association with First Edition Translations Ltd, Cambridge, UK
Editing by David Price in association with
First Edition Translations Ltd, Cambridge, UK
Typesetting by TheWriteIdea in association with
First Edition Translations Ltd, Cambridge, UK

Overall responsibility for production: h.f.ullmann publishing GmbH, Potsdam, Germany

Printed in China

ISBN 978-3-8480-0028-9

10 9 8 7 6 5 4 3 2 1
X IX VIII VII VI V IV III II I

www.ullmann-publishing.com
newsletter@ullmann-publishing.com

Bernhard Roetzel

A Guy's Guide to Style

h.f.ullmann

6 Foreword

8 Which rules still apply?

10 What do we mean by "business?"

64 Formal wear

80 Cool and casual

112 What we need

128 It's all about looking good

144 Shoes

170 How to buy efficiently

188 Accessories

206 Cleaning and care

220 Appendix

Foreword

More than ten years have now elapsed since my first book on men's fashion style was published. During this time, the world has changed either very little, dramatically, or not at all, depending on personal experience and general outlook. At first glance, the fashion world has undergone many changes.

Men have become more adventurous with regard to color. Clothes have, generally speaking, become more casual, and shorts, T-shirts and thongs are now standard wear in warm weather. The necktie has not disappeared altogether but it is worn less frequently nowadays. The suit has retained its importance while the sports jacket is experiencing a comeback.

The majority of men are still relatively uninterested in their appearance. Comfort is paramount. Clothes have to be practical without having to look particularly good. However, there is a growing body of younger men who are developing an interest in style and fashion. What is more, top designer brands are beginning to see them as a new, potential target group for suits, shirts and elegant shoes. Sneakers continue to dominate the scene but the leather shoe is back in force.

Over the past ten years, I have learned a lot about clothes, styles, fashion, and dress codes. While my enthusiasm for the subject has not diminished, I am now more convinced than ever that you cannot force someone to adopt a particular style. Individual tastes vary too much and people are too different. What I offer are suggestions, or I respond to the questions which crop up again and again.

I know that the majority of men do not take much interest in clothes, whereas some find the subject fascinating. In my experience, the greatest interest is often shown by very young men, many of whom are still at school or just beginning further training. They often take more of an interest in style and correct appearance than other more senior colleagues. These budding style experts are also particular about their leisure wardrobe. The suit is not the be-all and end-all of elegance.

The pleasure derived from wearing good clothes is one of the joys of living, as fashion and accessories are our daily companions. There are, of course, many other more important subjects in which you might become interested. But I cannot find many things of greater significance, because our relationship with clothes is such a close one. Cars can be fascinating, as can televisions, DVD players, clocks, and houses. But, unlike our clothes, none of these is ever in direct contact with us. So think carefully what you allow near you.

Bernhard Roetzel

Which rules

Given the fashion trends we actually see on the streets, the idea of special forums debating the loop behind the lapel on bespoke suits, designed to secure a boutonniere flower stem, must seem, to put it mildly, out of touch with real life. Similarly, ongoing debates about rules governing the pros and cons of brown or black shoes after 6 o'clock also appear far removed from reality, considering that 50 percent of men wear thongs in summer and the other 50 percent sneakers.

Do we need rules about what we should wear? Is there any point pondering the finer points of custom tailoring when 99 percent of the population buys ready-to-wear clothes as cheaply as possible? I believe there is. This is still a legitimate subject even if most people are not interested in it. After all, people still read books, even if everyone else only watches television, and they set the table, even though others have their meals on their laps (in front of the TV). Some things are worthwhile even if they have no specific purpose—one such example is the culture of clothes, the demise of which is frequently lamented: People now go to the opera wearing jeans, or visit an elegant restaurant without wearing a necktie, and often have no idea how to even tie a necktie.

Is it true that everything was better in the past? People certainly dressed more formally 100 years ago—at least in photos marking special occasions. The daily grind was often quite a different matter. However, even in the 1950s, it was still quite usual to spend as much as possible on one's wardrobe. And most people took great care to make sure that no button was ever lost and that shoes were always shiny. Meanwhile there was another, darker side to this coin: Many people simply could not afford new clothes, so they wore secondhand suits and overcoats. People in those days did not consider "secondhand" clothing chic or original.

still apply?

The culture of clothes also encompassed a respect for the craftsmen and –women working in the fashion industry—and perhaps the desire to wear hand-made clothing. Not everyone can afford such garments, however, and some people do not even want them. Rational reasons are often put forward in justification, namely that they last longer and are more comfortable to wear. The first point is only partly true. Even the

most expensive custom-made suit will quickly wear out if too much is expected of it. A moderately priced garment can last a long time if treated with care. As for being more comfortable, generally speaking this is true—but only if the valuable

garment fits well. In general, it is perhaps better to avoid too much rational thinking. Clothing is supposed to be fun.

In the business world, clothes are just one of many factors that can contribute to a person's success. First of all, you need qualifications. Secondly, it is important to be a good communicator. If these qualities are present, then the correct outfit is like the icing on the cake. Why allow your talents to be overlooked due to badly chosen clothes? You do not want to attract attention thanks to ill-fitting suits or strange pattern or color combinations.

(Left) A family occasion in 1906 would have required very formal attire. Even everyday clothes were more formal.
(Above) Nowadays, people only seem to wear comfortable clothes during leisure hours and rules only appear to apply to business attire and formal wear.

THE SUIT IS THE BUSINESS UNIFORM OF THE OFFICE WORKER
AND SIGNALS THE STATUS AND POSITION OF ITS WEARER.

What do we mean by "business?"

A good deal is talked about business fashion and there is no
shortage of style experts expounding their knowledge on the
subject on various websites and in seminars. Generally speaking, their comments refer to a code of dress which is only observed
in a limited number of business fields, such as banks, insurance
companies, law firms, and consultancy companies. We will be
discussing the fashion rules for these professions in this chapter. Other working environments have completely different
guidelines in this respect. People who work in research, for
example, or teachers, IT specialists, and sound engineers can
more or less wear what they like. They might well choose to
wear a suit and necktie but it would not be obligatory.

Have you ever found yourself in the financial district of a
big city around lunchtime? Restaurants and cafés tend to be packed with bankers dining on all kinds of delicacies, whether fast food or a more elaborate business meal. They
are identifiable from the way they are dressed: often a dark-gray suit, white shirt, necktie, and black shoes. However simple this description may sound at face value, there
are actually far more complicated issues at stake here. Business wear—in the sense
described here—is a uniform, which in turn implies standardization and recognizabil-
ity. Yet, for all its outward similarities, a uniform must also indicate distinctions in status. Military uniforms carry badges of rank but what happens in the business sector?
How does one distinguish between the business world's equivalents of sergeants, offi-
cers, and generals? The answer is that they, too, carry badges of office. Though perhaps
not as conspicuous as stars or stripes on epaulettes, they are unmistakable nonetheless.

Perfecting the art of business attire means wearing this uniform in the right way
while also conveying your position—at the correct level—within the hierarchy. Furthermore, a person's business outfit should also be an indication of where he is coming
from and, above all, where he is heading—information which can be gleaned from
details such as the cut and material of his suit, his necktie and shirt, his shoes and socks.

*The suit is one of the greatest design objects of the 20th century. Its basic shape has not altered since
the 1920s and remains fashionable to this day.*

The suit is the key

The suit is the foundation of a man's wardrobe. No single tailor or designer can claim sole responsibility for inventing this ensemble. Instead, it seems to have evolved gradually between the end of the 17th century and the 1930s, since when it has remained relatively unchanged. Any innovations have been limited to changes in the industrial manufacturing methods or the materials used. The latter have become lighter while, in recent years, the boundaries of what is still wearable seem to have been increasingly pushed to their limit. For daily office wear, delicate materials are quite simply unsuitable and suits of moderately heavy cloth remain the optimum choice.

The two most common types of suit today are the single-breasted suit, with two or three buttons, and the double-breasted suit. In the past, a vest used to be an essential feature of both of these but now it is the exception rather than the rule. The suit is generally the norm for men aged between 25 and 45 whereas older men tend to pre-

The majority of men only wear a suit to the office or for formal celebrations. This is a pity as a suit is extremely flattering.

fer a combination of blazer or jacket worn with contrasting pants, e.g. made in gray wool or light cotton. This type of combination is no real substitute for a suit but in many medium-sized firms, particularly in more provincial areas, it is more or less an accepted feature of the daily workplace. Even so, it inevitably gives off an air of provinciality. The fashion codes for people in offices tend to be British in origin since the United Kingdom is regarded as the capital of men's fashion. In accordance with the "no brown in town" dictum which was coined here, business suits used to be tailored in dark gray or blue. The reason for this was based primarily on practical considerations: Subdued tones were thought to be more practical in the grime and dirt of the city whereas browns and greens blended better with nature's palette in a rural setting. Designers have long since cast off the straitjacket of such fashion dictates and brown is nowadays an increasingly popular suit color. In an international context, however, brown is still not regarded as being entirely *comme il faut* for the office.

A suit must always be worn with a long-sleeved shirt. Millions of men may have other ideas in this respect but no matter how many of them opt to show bare forearms, this remains a basic fashion dictate. Whether this precept will ever be completely accepted, however, remains questionable. Most men—with the exception of senior management—insist on wearing short sleeves in summer—a stance which contradicts the original concept of the suit ensemble.

Like the spotless, white collar (from which the English expression "white-collar worker" originated), snow-white cuffs projecting from the sleeves of a suit used to be an office worker's trademark.

Basic rules for a formal business look

1 A dark, fine wool suit is the key element of the business look. It should be dark blue or dark gray in color. Brown and black are taboo as business wear.

2 The suit should be worn with a long-sleeved shirt with buttoned cuffs for everyday wear or double cuffs for special occasions (or even for everyday, if preferred). A soft button-down collar, the points of which can be buttoned down onto the shirt-front, has always been a classic style of business shirt, even if fashion experts or sales staff claim otherwise. This type of shirt is often considered too casual in some parts of Europe. And finally, a few words on what is apparently the favorite garment of many of the world's office workers: A short-sleeved shirt is fine if you are a bus driver or policeman but unsuitable attire for the office.

3 A jacket and pants are not acceptable business wear but might be worn on a Friday in the run-up to the weekend. This may not apply to middle-sized firms, freelance workers, or staff who have no direct contact with members of the general public. Navy-blue blazers are likewise unsuitable as business wear and were certainly never intended as such.

4 A necktie is an absolute must. This may change one day but for now a tie is as essential to a business outfit as a napkin is to an elegant meal. Different rules may apply in other business sectors where casual attire is the norm but these are not under discussion here.

5 Shoes must be black. The most formal shoes are those with closed lacing and as few perforated holes as possible, i.e. Oxford shoes. Brogues with a double leather sole are generally considered too crude to be worn with fine suits. Fashion purists regard loafers as too casual while buckled shoes are too dandyish. However, the important consideration here is color rather than style.

The custom of

ITALY Top executives can also be style icons—for example, Italian entrepreneur Luca di Montezemolo, who favors an extremely classic approach to fashion, such as a dark-blue double-breasted suit with light-blue shirt, complemented by a dark-blue necktie. Tip: A valuable Swiss watch is practically a must. Communication: The northern Italian work ethic is geared to efficiency and punctuality whereas southern Italians have a more casual approach. Be careful at business dinners—be sure to decline the offer of a second glass of wine or stick to water throughout.

USA As we know, Americans are extremely correct when it comes to business—and this should apply equally to your dress code. A suit and necktie should be considered compulsory. Many Americans will even apply this code in the evening, e.g. in sophisticated bars or fine restaurants and it is always a good idea to check the dress code of a restaurant when making a reservation. Manicured nails are considered normal among businessmen so do not hesitate to visit a men's nail salon prior to any important meetings. A positive attitude is essential at all times in business and this is enhanced if you take care of your appearance. If you are comfortable in your style of dress, you will soon be on first-name terms with new business associates.

GREAT BRITAIN Here the classic business look rules, even in summer, e.g. dark-blue suit with black lace-up shoes. Tip: Leave your striped neckties at home—the colors might be the special preserve of a college or upper-class club. Anyone wearing the exclusive, striped necktie without being a member would be awkwardly conspicuous (narrow light-blue stripes on black, for example, indicates the wearer is an Old Etonian). Communication: Understatement and self-mockery are a real asset. Even business speeches may be introduced with subtle humor.

the country

FRANCE Dark-gray suit, light-blue shirt, muted necktie. By day, medium- or even light-brown shoes are acceptable with a business suit, or even suede leather. Communication: English is the standard language but you will score points if you speak excellent French.

EASTERN EUROPE At senior levels, elegance is key: dark suit, white shirt, dark necktie. For the rest, the attitude to shirt sleeves is the same as it is elsewhere. Avoid red, as it can still have negative associations. Communication: East Europeans do not like being patronized so avoid any suggestion of lecturing. An important point about Poland and the Czech Republic is that people here regard themselves as Central Europeans. As far as they are concerned, Eastern Europe starts with Russia.

ASIA Classic, discreet. Special rules apply in Japan. Shoes must be removed when you enter a restaurant. For this reason, businessmen often carry a spare pair of socks in their briefcase. Threadbare socks should be discarded before the trip. Communication: Feelings are not shown openly. Behave quietly and show respect. Another important tip is that time in Japan is measured in seconds.

THE ISLAMIC WORLD A Western business look is standard. Clothes are generally kept buttoned and bare skin covered even after work—regardless of how hot it is. If the host removes his shoes on entering a room, be sure to do so too. Communication: Clocks here sometimes seem to run at a different rate so allow plenty of time. There is no need to fill pauses in conversation with small talk. Women are not a subject of conversation so refrain from polite enquiries about your host's wife or daughter.

The businessman in summer

A summer suit is a bit like the mythical Potemkin village. The aim is to preserve its outward appearance while keeping the man inside the suit as comfortable as possible despite the high temperatures. This is achieved largely by the type and weight of the fabric, which is measured in running meters. In Great Britain, around 9–11 oz (280–320 g) is considered "summer weight" whereas in Italy a fabric would not be classed as *leggero* unless it weighed 8 oz (230 g) or less. At a bespoke tailor's, the weight would be marked on the fabric swatches but if you are buying off the rack, you can only make an educated guess. Fabrics marked "Super 100 S" or "Super 180 S," however, have nothing to do with the fabric weight but merely classify the grades of the fibers from which the material is woven. The higher the number, the finer the fabric. The highest S-numbered fabric currently considered suitable for daily wear is Super 150 S.

Fabric experts will also examine the weave of a material. The more loosely the threads are interwoven, the better the ventilation. Extremely lightweight fabrics made from heavily twisted thread are often densely woven, which makes them crease-resistant but less light and airy. Consequently, a heavier fabric may actually feel less warm in hot weather in the same way as a polo shirt made of cotton piqué, a much thicker fabric than shirt material, is nonetheless more comfortable to wear in hot weather. If you have an opportunity to look at the fabric before ordering the suit, hold it up to the light and check the openness of the weave.

These weight values apply to fabrics made from animal fibers, such as wool or cashmere. Cotton and linen are often substantially heavier yet feel cooler on the skin. They do crease badly, however, so are not really ideal for daily wear. The dress code does permit cotton for daily business wear and also permits an exception from the "no brown in town" rule. Classic shades include tobacco, café au lait, khaki, olive, and stone. Wool is still a more suitable option for important meetings, ideally in blue or gray. White suits are taboo in the business sector unless you are running your company from a villa in Capri. In the USA it is perfectly acceptable for brokers and

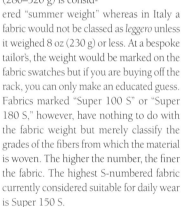

bankers to wear suits made of seersucker, this fabric would be regarded as rather strange if it were seen at Frankfurt's stock exchange. Linen may well be a delightful fabric but it is better suited to leisurewear.

The lighter the material, the more delicate it is. The legendary long life of elderly, custom-made suits is largely due to what were—compared to contemporary fabric—incredibly heavy grades of cloth. Forty years ago, 21 oz/yd (600 g/m) would not have been unusual for an outdoor suit. Nowadays, only winter coats at most would be made of such a sartorial heavyweight. Materials which contain a mix of synthetics are simultaneously lightweight and hard-wearing. Traditional tailoring turns up its nose at such fabrics but in hot, humid climates it is considered perfectly normal to have a business wardrobe tailored from cashmere mixed with synthetic fibers. Weaving companies have a wide range of materials available for such markets but the Europeans remain reluctant customers in this respect. A devotee of natural fibers can opt for mohair for his travel wardrobe. This faintly shiny fabric, made from goat hair, was very popular in the Sixties, but subsequently became reserved mainly for evening dress and tuxedos. Nowadays, the silvery sheen of this exceedingly elastic material is once again popular with designers.

The British have a reputation for being incapable of manufacturing lightweight suits. For a long time, this was indeed the case and was due to the tra-

ditional, heavy horsehair interfacing used to give the jacket shape across the chest. The Italian practice is to back the outer fabric with just a thin linen underlay—producing a garment which feels "shirt-like" to wear. Furthermore, the inner lining is pared down to a minimum, which makes the suit even more light and airy. Half-lined suits of this kind are as popular in the USA as they are in Italy. In other parts of Europe, however, customers remain unconvinced—perhaps because a garment which is not fully lined looks unfinished.

A lightweight suit sets the tone for the rest of the outfit. A silver-gray suit made from a cool wool-and-mohair mix would ideally be teamed with a white Swiss voile shirt and a narrow, black necktie of fine knitted cotton. It goes without saying that

the shirt should be long-sleeved—a short-sleeved shirt would simply be wrong. Even in a tropical climate, knee-high socks are a must. The most comfortable option would be a very thin, extra-fine mix of wool and silk. Heavy brogues should remain in the shoe cupboard and a looser style of loafer worn instead.

Quality check when purchasing a suit

1 When buying a suit, remember the price-quality equation: not much money = not much quality, lots of money = lots of quality. Exceptions to this rule include designer garments (too expensive) and sale items (maximum quality at minimum cost, especially if an elegant boutique is having a stock clearance). And what may one expect

from the various price categories? 200 dollars may buy you a suit from a discount store. You should only consider a cheaper option if it comes from somewhere like H&M, which at least offers good design at a modest price. However, the fabric and finish will not be all that good. If you are lucky, 700 dollars will buy you an acceptable suit but you may need to spend up to 2000 dollars to get high-class workmanship in a top-quality fabric.

TIP: Either opt for a very cheap suit, or else spend a decent amount of money on the purchase. The middle price bracket offers the least value for money in terms of price and quality.

2 What does the label reveal? It is worth reading the label as this contains valuable information on the origin of the

fabric. If it cites the name of the firm, the garment will be an own-brand product. It may not be quite as prestigious as a designer label, but it often offers a good price-quality ratio (although the price categories mentioned in Point 1 still apply). If the garment carries the name of a famous designer, you would probably have to spend too much —especially if the designer is not normally associated with suits or menswear. Alternatively, the label might be that of a ready-to-wear producer, indicating that the suit comes directly from the manufacturer.

TIP: Buying a manufacturer's brand name is usually the best solution, as this does not involve a famous name cashing in on licensing charges or getting a cut in some other way. And, if something is not right, you know where to return it.

3 What kind of fabric is it? However beautifully tailored a suit may be, the end result can never be as good if the fabric itself does not justify the workmanship involved. It is usually possible to tell the quality of a fabric just by feeling it with your fingertips. Really good-quality material feels better to the touch: softer,

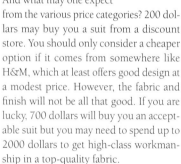

smoother, finer—simply more agreeable. Cheap fabric, on the other hand, feels scratchy, stiff, and rough. Just carry out a comparison by placing the cheapest suit in the range next to the most expensive and feel the difference.

It is also useful to read the small print. A label on the inside pocket contains all the relevant data concerning the suit, including its size, model number, cut, and the fabric code number. This is only useful in the event of a customer complaint. As far as quality is concerned, it is information such as "100% pure new wool" or "80% pure new wool, 10% silk, 10% cashmere" which is of key interest. Most importantly, avoid suits made of synthetic fibers at all costs! Even linings should not be made of nylon or similar synthetic materials. One exception to this rule: Lightweight fabrics may contain small amounts of synthetic fibers to prevent creasing.

TIP: The minimum you should aim for is "pure new wool," meaning that the fibers have come from the shorn animal and spun into yarn for the first time. The designation "pure wool," on the other hand, means that the yarn has been recycled from old garments and fiber residues.

4 Workmanship. First, turn the pants inside out. The better the suit, the more elegant the workmanship. By all means, check the knee lining as well: Cheaper suits will often have nylon lining, which can cause excessive perspiration. As for the jacket, check whether the stripes run down through the breast pocket without interruption. A square pattern should run in a continuous horizontal line from the chest across to the sleeve. The degree of accuracy in the pattern match reflects the quality of the suit. Paying 2000 dollars or more should guarantee you hand-sewn buttonholes, buttons made from natural materials, and sewn-in interfacing (i.e. it is stitched to the outer fabric instead of simply being glued in place).

TIP: How to tell if the interfacing is hand-basted. Firstly, you should be able to feel the interfacing at waist level as a third, loose layer of fabric. Secondly, in good-quality garments, the fine, hand-basted stitches used to attach the interfacing should be visible underneath the collar.

The business trip

A business trip is merely normal life lived under more difficult conditions. Your choice of clothing shrinks in proportion to the size of a wardrobe that is reduced to the limits of your suitcase. If you normally have between five and 50 suits to choose from each morning, you can only expect to have one to three options available during your hotel sojourn. This requires some careful, forward planning and avoiding of risks.

Hard-sided suitcases provide maximum protection for your clothes—should your baggage end up in Mombasa instead of Milan. It also provides sufficient room for two to three outfits complete with all the necessary accessories.

Smaller cases or bags on wheels with telescopic handles have been the norm for short trips. These can, at a push, also accommodate a suit but ideally they should be reserved for spare shirts and a wash bag.

The clothes brush—a vital accessory for business trips. Dark suits inevitably attract dust and fluff, and a brush is the best remedy in such circumstances. Sticky rollers are not recommended as they may harm the fabric.

Large clothes bags are frequently used for business travel although I, personally, do not favor them. They offer no protection against crushing and are awkward to handle whether they are folded or unfolded. They are really only practical for car journeys.

An overnight or weekend bag accommodates just enough clothing for a short trip away. This option is ideal for conveying resilient sportswear.

For example, anyone banking on wearing the same suit two days in a row, thereby requiring only a change of shirt and necktie, can easily come to grief. All it takes is a careless stewardess to spill tomato juice everywhere or a pigeon to drop a biological bomb as it flies overhead. How extremely inconvenient if there is no dry-cleaner available nearby! Far better, therefore, to take the precaution of packing some spare suits. Although you can save time by only carrying hand luggage, you may find it worthwhile to take a suitcase with a much more extensive wardrobe along instead: Having to purchase new clothes under pressure at your destination or have them dry-cleaned may end up eating up even more of your precious time.

Neckties for your trip

PACK NECKTIES WITH GREAT CARE SO THAT THEY ARE NOT CREASED UPON ARRIVAL.

The first method involves winding the necktie around your hand and placing it in a corner of your luggage where it will not get squashed. In method two, the rolled-up necktie is placed inside the neck of a shirt. Method three requires folding the necktie in half lengthwise and laying it on top. Alternatively, it can be placed on the bottom of the suitcase where it will remain flat. A fourth option is to purchase a special necktie travel case. One way or another, it is prudent to take several neckties along on business trips. Apart from anything else, a necktie could be put out of action as a result of becoming stained. In order to minimize this risk, some travelers prefer to take dark neckties along on their travels since small marks remain relatively inconspicuous. It is also wise to opt for neckties made of somewhat less delicate Jacquard silk so that splashes can, if necessary, be removed with the blade of a knife.

Custom-made suits for the office

Custom-made clothing and business attire do not automatically go together. However, most men do at least have their business suits custom-made, because it is, after all, an excellent idea. Although it is true that clothes are no substitute for efficiency, they do nevertheless create the impression of competence. Anyone who is very good at his job but has no idea about clothes will seem less competent than someone who is well-dressed.

There are several types of made-to-measure clothing. The simplest, though least personalized, involves individually ordering a standard size of suit in a desired fabric. The retailer will, for example, order a suit in dark-gray flannel in the size of your choice. He will not take any measurements but will make minor alterations to the finished garment—to the waistband or sleeve length, for example. This option is foolproof and useful if a standard size provides a good fit. Only a few manufacturers offer this service, however, but it is still worth enquiring. Custom-made clothing is certainly a more personalized option but is still beset with uncertainties. Standard sizes are used as a starting-point here too, but the basic pattern, which is closest to the person's shape, is then customized. Working on the basis of a size 42, for example, the chest size, back width, jacket length, waist and seat measurements, sleeve length and waistband (in the case of

Only handmade suits are still cut out by hand using shears, as shown here at this London outfitters.

pants), leg length, and width can all be adjusted. As a rule, the garment is fashioned from a standardized base pattern rather than measurements taken of the body itself. This helps to avoid any misinterpretation of the size of the garment. The chest measurement, for example, can vary considerably, depending on whether a snug- or loose-fitting jacket is required.

A hand-made suit offers the greatest individuality. However, it also carries the greatest risk of disappointment. The tailor will construct a cutting pattern to fit the client's shape, which reflects his measurements and style preferences. During the construction process, however, these measurements may—to a greater or lesser degree—fail to live up to the client's original requirements, thanks to the tailor's own preferences or cutting system. Let us assume, for example, that the client orders a double-breasted suit with three sets of buttons, two straight side pockets with flaps, and a pair of double-pleated pants with cuffs. The tailor takes out his tape measure and constructs a model. In a worst-case scenario, the client may discover at the first fitting that his double-breasted suit bears no resemblance to what he had in mind. In other words, the same sketch of a suit, if ordered from ten different tailors, could produce ten fundamentally different garments. For this reason, custom tailoring is only recommended if you are clear about your requirements and can describe them accurately in words or, better still, in sketches—and if the tailor is competent and stylish enough to comprehend your wishes and turn them into reality. Good tailors are usually able to do this, but the incompetent ones simply ignore their clients' ideas.

To sum up: Ready-to-wear was conceived in order to be able to produce clothes more cheaply and have them ready on demand. There is basically nothing wrong with ready-to-wear: Far better to get a well-fitting, ready-to-wear suit, which is properly constructed and finished, than an expensive disaster from the custom-made sector. Finding a tailor who understands you and who also produces good workmanship is almost as difficult as finding the right partner in life but sometimes it does all come together and you really do get lucky.

The only sour note is the exorbitantly high price you have to pay for the privilege. Custom tailors in the US will often not get their tape measures out for anything less than about 2500 dollars. It is not uncommon for a suit to cost between

4000 and 8000 dollars. These figures would cause most people to catch their breath. But the price does, after all, take account

A luxury suiting fabric can sweeten even the most mundane working day in the office.

of the 60 or so hours of hand-finishing that goes into the construction of such a garment. Still, it is reasonable to wonder whether a suit for 4000 dollars is indeed ten times better than a suit which costs 400 dollars. Cost notwithstanding, this is a question that every individual must answer for himself. The legendary Rolls Royce cars had a thin line on the side of the bodywork painted by hand. Some people felt this was important, while others opted instead for a Mercedes. The same thing is true of custom tailoring. Anyone who needs to have the beauty of a hand-made buttonhole explained to him would be advised to buy clothes off the rack.

The business shirt

A white shirt suggests involvement in the sort of pursuits that do not involve getting your fingers dirty. People in other countries prefer to team a suit with a light-blue shirt, a color which is generally flattering to the male complexion. Internationally speaking, pink is also still considered an acceptable color for office wear. But in many countries men in white shirts are still a familiar sight—be it at the airport, at lunchtime in one of the restaurants around the downtown business district, or behind the wheel of a station wagon (with their jackets hanging neatly on a clothes hanger behind the driver's seat). Striped or checked patterns are, of course, perfectly acceptable: the more delicate the pattern, the more formal the shirt. The most popular styles are those that look a uniform light blue when viewed from a distance. The British passion for extremely loud stripes or extra large checks is generally not shared elsewhere. In Italy and France, big patterns like this are not considered elegant enough for office wear. A shirt with a contrasting white collar is a good compromise between the simple white shirt and other shades and designs. However, this style is still associated to its detriment with the yuppies from the Eighties. If you do not want to invite criticism of the clothes you wear, it would be best to avoid a contrasting collar. As far as shirt style is concerned, the most acceptable options are any variation of the cutaway collar. It should be stressed once again at this point that the American button-down collar is perfectly suitable for office wear. There are good reasons why it

Business shirt fabrics

The top cotton fabrics comprise full-twist quality Egyptian fiber material. Full-twist means that warp and weft—in other words, the cross- and lengthwise threads of the weave—are made of twisted yarn. "Twisted" means that two or more strands of fiber are spun under tension into a thread. In high-quality garments, color is always considered in conjunction with the thread. A light-blue shirt is therefore woven from

is popular with such international managers as Luca di Montezemolo.

Cuffs should be fastened with buttons. Where there are two or more buttons, these should be aligned one above the other, not next to each other.

The ability to make the cuff tighter or wider is a classic concession to the ready-to-wear market. If your shirts are not custom-made, the buttons will be sited so that the cuffs fasten precisely around the wrist. Double cuffs are more formal and obviously never turned round the wrong way, and they require cuff links. These elegant accessories should never be forgotten when traveling.

Traditionalists prefer shirts without breast pockets as these were not originally part of a shirt's design. What is the point of them anyway? In the past, when suits automati-

cally included a vest, there were enough places to keep things in, but the shirt pocket is now intended to provide a substitute. However, if you do not have a pocket, you will not be tempted to keep your cell phone or pen in it.

Monograms are actually a perfectly normal addition to a shirt. However, many men feel that embroidered initials suggest an excess of vanity. Anyone who wants to personalize his shirts in this way would be better advised, therefore, to conceal his initials inside his jacket. Located a hand's width to the left of the navel, they will not be immediately visible. In my opinion, this is the best location of all. A monogram visible on a shirt-front would resemble a designer logo, and would not look very elegant on a shirt cuff.

light-blue yarn. Patterned shirts are woven from several thread colors. This makes the fabric colorfast, even in areas that get a lot of wear. Cheap shirts, on the other hand, tend to fade around the edges. In addition to their silky feel and elegant sheen, top-quality shirt fabrics also have the additional advantage of minimal shrinkage and a long life.

The qualities of fiber and yarn are objective criteria; how the fabric feels is due to the final finishing process, which gives the fabric, fresh off the loom and as rough as a scouring cloth, the desired "feel." Poplin should be fairly silky, batiste or voile

should be light and airy, and Oxford should be coarsely hard-wearing. The fabric is initially placed in a gigantic washing machine, then spun and dried in a giant mangle with heated rollers. Its surface is then smoothed during later finishing stages and acquires its sought-after elegant sheen.

Non-iron fabrics are particularly popular among many customers. Ironing will only be successful if the manufacturer's care instructions are carefully followed.

Collar designs

The collar is practically the most important part of the shirt, since its shape determines how good an impression our appearance makes. Unfortunately, this aspect of a shirt is completely neglected by most men. This is partly due to the widespread misconceptions regarding the correct shape of a shirt. Many sales staff claim that the collar is a correct fit if you can still insert one or two fingers between it and the neck. More often than not, however, collars end up being much too wide if this criterion is observed. Better advice would be that the collar should fit snugly around the neck without being too tight.

A collar which is too wide will make the wearer look either too thin or even ill, as if poor health has led to a loss of weight. Secondly, a collar which is too wide leaves too much of the neck exposed and detracts from the formality. Thirdly, a necktie which is too wide will leave the collar wrinkled.

Fashion is constantly varying the shape of the collar, changing the height and dimensions of the collar sides. However, the basic forms remain the same: The more cutaway are the collar tips, the more elegant the effect. And the higher up the neck it sits, the more formal it looks. Accordingly, a high cutaway collar is still the best

Cutaway collar: elegant with a suit but also looks good without a necktie.

The Kent or classic spread collar is versatile and still the most popular collar design.

option to wear with a suit. The lightest style of collar is the button-down collar, the tips of which button onto the shirt front. This is supposed to prevent them flying up during a game of polo. The New York firm of Brooks Brothers, allegedly inspired by English polo players, claims to have invented this type of collar. Consequently, this type of collar is still called a "polo collar" at Brooks Brothers to this day. In America, button-down collared shirts are accepted partners to a business suit. In parts of Europe, however, many retailers and image consultants believe this style should be reserved for

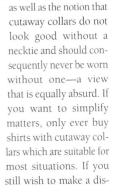

leisurewear. But many men feel they know better and are prepared to ignore this view, as well as the notion that cutaway collars do not look good without a necktie and should consequently never be worn without one—a view that is equally absurd. If you want to simplify matters, only ever buy shirts with cutaway collars which are suitable for most situations. If you still wish to make a distinction between work and leisure time, you can wear cutaway collars with your suit, and button-down shirts with your casual outfit.

White shirt with cutaway collar: the classic business shirt.

The button-down collar with a soft roll.

The best collars

The classic English cutaway collar. (All images in this section supplied by Emanuel Berg).

A cutaway collar with more widely spread collar tips displays more of the necktie knot.

A slightly smaller, cutaway collar with a relatively gentle spread displays a thicker knot best.

The most elegant collar style is a very widely spread, cutaway collar which is not too high.

Large and soft: a button-down collar in the Italian style.

The tab collar looks particularly smart as it forms a snug fit around the necktie knot.

at a glance

In the 1940s, collar tips were worn closer together. Good with a bow tie.

Men with a long neck should wear a higher collar with two buttons.

A wide, cutaway, relatively large collar can make a large face appear smaller.

A collar with rounded tips always looks somewhat dandyish.

A tab collar with rounded tips and a pin is not a style for shrinking violets.

The high, wing-tip collar is now only worn with an evening suit. It was formerly also worn with morning dress.

Shirts and their fabrics:

Batiste A light plain weave using fine, high-quality yarns.

Cotton Fiber made from the seed hairs of the cotton plant, which thrives in tropical and sub-tropical conditions.

Cotton flannel A soft quality, plain, or twill weave, usually used for leisurewear shirts.

Cotton twill A hardwearing fabric in twill weave, mainly used for leisurewear shirts.

End-on-end Shirt fabrics which consist of two warp yarns in different colors, which are interwoven, creating a characteristic multicolored effect (this is also known as "Fil-à-fil").

Fil-à-fil Cf. End-on-end.

Finishing A finishing technique after weaving to improve the look and "hand" (feel) of a fabric.

Full-twist fabrics are woven with warp and weft of twisted yarns. They are considered the ultimate choice for formal shirts.

Gingham check A fine shirt check, usually either in a pale blue/white or pink/white combination.

Half linen A mixed fabric consisting of 50% linen and 50% cotton which is less prone to creasing than pure linen.

Half-twist fabric This is when a twisted yarn is used only for the weft. It is considered a lower quality material. Nevertheless, half-twist fabrics are often less likely to crease and are soft to wear.

Linen A light, cool fabric made from the fibers of the flax plant. It is seldom used for business shirts as it creases easily.

Mako cotton An Egyptian brand of cotton, which provides high-quality thread, e.g. for batiste.

Marcella (or piqué) A type of fabric with a waffle-like weave which is sometimes used for the chest, collar, and cuffs of traditional formal evening shirts.

Non-iron Easycare fabrics which do not need to be ironed. This only works if the manufacturer's instructions are followed.

Oxford is a coarser kind of weave, spun with warp and weft strands of yarns dyed in different colors. This creates a lustrous, multicolored effect.

Pinpoint is a more refined version of Oxford cloth and is woven with warp and weft threads in various colors.

Poplin is the term for fabrics in plain weave which use far more warp than weft threads. It is classed as single, half-twist or full-twist poplin depending on the yarn used.

a glossary of terms

Roman stripes are broad stripes used for business shirts, e.g. dark blue on white.

Sea Island cotton is the finest type of cotton from the Caribbean. In the 19th century, some of the best Egyptian cotton plants were cultivated from its seeds.

Shrink-resistant means that a fabric is liable to only minimal shrinkage. Top-quality weaving mills guarantee a shrinkage of no more than 1.5%.

Tattersall check is a multi-colored check pattern on a light background, traditionally used for leisurewear shirts.

Twill is a fabric characterized by a pattern of diagonal parallel ribs. It is hard-wearing and popular for sports shirts.

Twist is produced by twisting several yarns. This process strengthens the fabric and so reduces creasing.

Vichy is a small check pattern either in a plain or twill weave, e.g. in a light-blue/white combination.

Voile is a sheer and semitransparent fabric which is used for formal evening shirts or extremely lightweight summer shirts.

Warp and weft Cloth is produced by inter-weaving threads lengthwise and crosswise (cf. weave). The warp is the set of lengthwise yarns, whereas the yarn which runs over and under the warp threads is called the weft or fill.

Weave is a method in which warp and weft are inter-woven. There are three basic types of weave: plain, twill, and Atlas.

Yarn is made by twisting fiber strands together to form a thread.

Zephir is a very fine, densely woven fabric, usually very light and available in pastel shades.

(Below) Scabal deliver high-quality bespoke shirts from their extensive range of fabrics.

A custom-made business shirt

Manufacturers of custom-made shirts frequently claim in their advertising that a personally tailored shirt will give the wearer an incomparable feeling of individuality and luxury, not to mention a far better fit. It goes without saying that custom-made shirts should be a good fit but the degree to which they fit better than ordinary ready-to-wear shirts depends largely on the shape of the wearer. The quality of material in custom-made shirts is not automatically better. A cheap producer will obviously use cheap fabrics. Such fabrics are frequently of poorer quality than those used by good ready-to-wear shirt manufactur-

ers, who often buy in bulk in order to be able to sell at a competitive price. Even with custom-made shirts, you will get exactly what you pay for.

A shirt-maker producing a garment by hand will, generally speaking, take the same measurements as are required for a jacket (in other words, chest size, back width, arm length, waist and hip measurements, back length). From these, he will construct a pattern that will then be cut out, initially out of white linen rather than the final fabric itself. Using this, he will sew a prototype of the shirt with a collar and cuffs made of card.

A large choice of collar styles and fabrics.

The watch should fit perfectly underneath the cuff of the custom-made shirt.

The sleeve should be measured in such a way that the cuff extends beyond the jacket sleeve.

Only after the client has tried the sample garment on will the tailor risk using his shears on the actual cloth. The advantage of this is that if the cut turns out to be completely wrong, it is only the cheap prototype that must be discarded and not an expensive fabric. The disadvantage lies in the fact that fittings cost time and money. Tailors who work with shirt manufacturing firms and shirt-makers with their own production facilities approach the task in different ways. They keep a selection of sample shirts in every conceivable size, sometimes in various basic cuts, e.g. a looser cut will suit some men's tastes, whereas a more figure-hugging version is favored by others. They will also have a fairly wide choice of collar styles and cuff designs.

The client will try on a shirt in his size and one of the sales staff will measure the extent to which it will have to be adjusted in order to fit the client's shape and figure. In this respect, the procedure is similar to ordering a customized ready-to-wear suit.

Finally, the client chooses a collar and cuffs and decides on details such as the style and number of folds on the sleeves and rear yoke, whether or not to include a breast pocket, straight or curving bottom seams, the shape and position of a breast pocket, if so desired, and, of course, the fabric. If the shirt fits and meets with approval, this sample can be saved for all future orders. Unlike suits, the fit of which can, despite identical measurements, vary astonishingly depending on the fabric used, any subsequent shirts will have exactly the same fit. Variations in the weight of shirt fabrics are too minimal to affect the way it fits. The system does, however, depend on the shirt manufacturer not altering his cut.

Neck and chest circumference are measured on the body and the shirt measurements are then worked out to the client's wishes.

The back measurement determines the total length of the shirt. The customer's wishes are important.

The necktie

The necktie is the symbol of the business world and an exclusively male accessory. Some designers occasionally argue the case for women to wear a necktie but it would look as misplaced on a woman as a dress would on a man. For several years, there has been a growing tendency to dispense with the necktie whenever the opportunity is offered. It does, however, add the finishing touch to the business look. The main points to remember are:

1 Neckties should ideally be made of pure silk—a synthetic fabric is out of the question. Other natural fibers, such as cashmere, wool, cotton, linen, or any silk-linen mix are, of course, also perfectly acceptable. However, none of these

The striped necktie
Stripes were originally a sign of membership, perhaps of a school, college, regiment, or club. Nowadays, the majority of striped neckties no longer reflect this.

The spotted necktie
The spotted necktie is an English classic worn with a business suit. It can easily be worn with a striped or check shirt provided that the size of the pattern is different.

The knitted necktie
Silk knitted neckties can theoretically be worn with a business suit but most people find them something of a curiosity. Perhaps they should just be worn for important meetings.

alternatives is necessary for an average business day. Wool neckties, for example, may indeed look wonderfully Italian but would be something of a curiosity to most of your colleagues.

2 The best type of knot is what is known as the Four-in-Hand. All versions of the Windsor knot produce a knot that is much too big—its V-shape does not easily fit into a shirt collar. There are many alternative knots, but these are completely unnecessary, apart from the "small knot."

This is an excellent knot, ideal for very tall men since it uses only a small amount of necktie.

3 A necktie is designed for decorative purposes and its primary task is to coordinate the shirt and jacket. However, the space between the lapel, pants, and shirt collar positively cries out to be filled. A suit and shirt may well look cool, but can easily seem incomplete, like a table set without napkins.

The themed necktie
Themed neckties are rather controversial and would be frowned upon by many style advisors. The important element is the motif on the necktie. Naked women are somewhat problematical but naked elephants, on the other hand, are perfectly acceptable.

The marinella necktie
Italians, so famed for their elegant fashion sense, tend to prefer a more muted, discreet design for office wear. It is advisable to emulate them in this respect, as a necktie should never be too prominent.

The single-color necktie
A single-colored necktie can provide an oasis of calm, especially when worn with a strongly patterned shirt. A long dark-blue necktie is a particularly versatile and attractive choice and, with a light-colored shirt, is also ideal for television appearances.

The necktie: what it signals

SINGLE-COLOR NECKTIES are available in every possible shade and color and numerous types of weave. The single color certainly simplifies the issue of matching the necktie to a shirt. A plain, dark-blue Jacquard silk necktie was the understated preference of style icon Gianni Agnelli.

What does the dress code say? Office: yes, e.g. in navy blue or wine red. Elegant dining: yes—lighter colors also acceptable. Special occasions: yes, e.g. in muted blues and reds. Smart weekend look: yes, e.g. in rust brown or green.

STRIPED NECKTIES signal that the wearer has a distinct affinity with Anglo-Saxon fashion style. They also permit a conservatively dressed man to make a personal statement through his choice of bright, bold colors.

What does the dress code say? Office: yes—preferably in muted color combinations for important meetings. Elegant dining: yes—all colors are acceptable. Special occasions: yes, but in muted colors. Smart weekend look: yes—in country combinations of green, wine red, brown, or yellow.

SPOTTED NECKTIES A timeless classic. The rule of thumb is: the bigger the spots, the bolder the effect. Classic color combinations consist of white spots on a dark-blue or bright-red background. Tiny white dots on pink or pale yellow are also suitable for summer wear.

What does the dress code say? Office: yes, e.g. in dark blue or black with white polka dots. Elegant dining: yes—a paler background color is also acceptable depending on the season. Special occasions: yes, but only with small pinhead dots on a dark background. Smart weekend look: no.

PAISLEY is regarded as a typically British design but it is actually of Oriental origin. The wildly swirling patterns based on fertility symbols are seen to best effect on fine matte silk. Paisley neckties are acceptable business wear provided the design is elegant and the colors are appropriate for the office, such as wine red or dark blue. A sports jacket can also be teamed with a Paisley necktie in strong shades of brown, green, or yellow.

What does the dress code say? Office: only muted and elegant designs acceptable. Elegant dining: yes—even strong reds and yellows are permissible. Special occasions: yes, but preferably in more muted colors. Smart weekend look: yes—as this is the natural setting for a Paisley design.

GEOMETRICAL DESIGNS Some of these are so cleverly woven that they almost appear three-dimensional, while others shimmer dizzyingly. Such illusional effects can make this style of necktie a real eye-catcher but try to avoid imposing excessively hypnotic designs on your opposite number at the negotiating table.

and what the dress code says

What does the dress code say? Office: yes, but opt for a fairly conservative design. Elegant dining: yes, but avoid overly obtrusive versions which will distract your table companion. Special occasions: yes—especially on a silver-colored background, for example. Smart weekend look: no.

THEMED NECKTIES are available to cater for all tastes, ranging from kitsch to art. If your taste runs to this style of necktie, be sure to exercise some caution in your choice. A giant cactus in garish green may be highly amusing but will merely attract skeptical looks in a business environment.

What does the dress code say? Office: not a good idea. Elegant dining: yes, but with a fairly discreet motif. Special occasions: no. Smart weekend look: no.

FANTASY NECKTIE DESIGNS Floral, organically flowing, tiny or huge—fantasy designs allow fashion designers to give full vent to their creative expression, which is why a "designer necktie" is somewhat frowned upon by those who favor a classic wardrobe. Some designers create designs with one main purpose in mind: to attract attention. Conservative necktie wearers, on the other hand, generally seek to avoid it.

What does the dress code say? Office: not usually in conservative business sectors. Elegant dining: yes, depending on personal taste. Special occasions: no. Smart weekend look: no.

SCOTTISH TARTANS This covers a wide area as there are hundreds of different patterns. Italian men wear a plaid necktie with a dark business suit. In Great Britain, however, this would be a faux pas, as tartan neckties are the exclusive preserve of country living. Elsewhere, they signal a sense of individuality.

What does the dress code say? Office: yes—albeit only a "quiet" tartan, such as the Blackwatch pattern. Elegant dining: yes—stronger colors would also be acceptable. Special occasions: no. Smart weekend look: yes—ideally in earthy, natural colors.

GLEN PLAID, SHEPHERD'S PLAID, HERRINGBONE etc. Many jacket designs are often echoed in necktie form, usually in Jacquard fabrics. Since most of these are based on extremely complex patterns, they work best when teamed with a single-color shirt and a large-patterned suit. Classic example: a gray Glen-plaid necktie with a white shirt and a dark-gray, pin-striped worsted suit.

What does the dress code say? Office: yes—provided that the pattern is small on a blue, wine-red, or silver-gray background. Elegant dining: yes, in similar colors as for office wear. Special occasions: yes, e.g. a fine Glen plaid or shimmering Shepherd's plaid. Smart weekend look: yes—albeit a larger pattern on a brown or green background.

Some facts about silk

Silk was already being produced in China in 2640 BC. Chinese silk reached Persia in around 400 BC and arrived in Lower Asia and Egypt about 200 years later. This exotic fabric did not arrive in Europe until the last century BC. Under the Romans, silk quickly became a sought-after luxury item. Its exclusive quality remained unchanged—even when the Arabs began to produce silk of their own during the 8th century and the technique spread from 10th-century Sicily throughout the rest of the Italian peninsula.

By the Middle Ages, silk was either being produced, traded, or processed practically all over the known world, but it was the Florentines who dominated this branch of the textile industry in the 17th century. The French then took over as leading silk producers, as this delicate fabric became the first choice for the haut monde and a must at court. At the end of the 18th century the English penchant for wool and cotton in men's fashion began to gain ground but silk did not completely disappear from the scene as a result. It was reserved for vests, dressing-gowns, and socks, or used for linings.

The artistically fashioned neckties of the 19th-century dandy were not initially made of silk but of snow-white linen or fine lace. It was not until the late 1880s that silk came to be regarded as sufficiently decorative to be worn as an accessory around the neck. This was partly due to the accelerating pace of industrialization and the ensuing opportunities for the mass production of the once rare silk fabrics. The geometrical allover designs emanating from

Macclesfield in England quickly proved very popular with a male clientele, as did the Oriental-style Paisley designs from the Scottish town of that name, which has been spinning silk fibers grown in British colonies since the 18th century and weaving them into Indian designs which still retain an exotic appeal to this day.

The basic principle of silk production has not really changed significantly since the early days. It continues to be an rather time-consuming and labor-intensive procedure. As soon as the silk worms have finished wrapping themselves up in a cocoon of silk, the pupae are killed using either hot vapor or hot air. The cocoons are then soaked in water to remove the

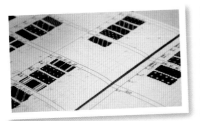

sticky substance which glued the threads together. The threads, which are unwound with the aid of brushes, can be over 3280 yards (3000 m) long, although only 328 to 875 yards (300–800 m) of this will be of suitable quality for making high-grade raw silk. Before the silk can be spun or woven, any remnants of the sticky glue have to be removed by boiling it in a soap solution—a process known as "boiling off."

China is still the biggest supplier of high-grade raw silk. However, the world center for producing neckties from silk fabrics is the northern Italian city of Como. Local firms there carry out the entire process, from designing the patterns to finishing the end product. The silk is either printed or woven into Jacquard from various colored silk threads. Silk printing is particularly suited for pictorial or floral designs as this procedure can capture any motif in all its detail on the fabric. Woven silk, on the other hand, is mainly used for geometrical and rhythmical patterns, which are best created by warp and weft.

Even experienced experts find it difficult to assess the quality of silk accurately. Visually, it is almost impossible to distinguish between a synthetic fabric and genuine silk, which is why a sense of touch is such an important factor when assessing the quality. The most obvious difference between genuine silk and a synthetic alternative is that the chemical imposter produces much smoother threads and, consequently, fabrics with a much silkier feel. The necktie should, therefore, be allowed to slide through your fingers. Genuine silk will snag on the tiniest rough bit of skin or sharp fingernail, whereas imitation silk will slide over it unchecked.

One further, frequently recommended quality test is to crush the fabric in your hand. A good-quality product will survive such treatment without any permanent creasing. Caution should be exercised, however, if the necktie in question is still the property of the retailer at this stage. Various other quality-control techniques, such as singeing the fabric, are clearly unsuitable options for the potential purchaser. He must, therefore, rely on the quality guarantee inherent in the brand of necktie. A good name generally insures good quality and the corresponding price should provide a useful guideline in this respect. You will not find top-quality products for less than a certain minimum price level.

The four-in-hand

Despite the large number of necktie knots, most men actually get by with three basic knots. The most important of these is the so-called simple knot or four-in-hand knot, which is suitable for all neckties and collars. The four-in-hand knot is a longish knot. The width of the necktie's middle section determines the precise thickness. Place the necktie around your neck with the broader end on your right. It must hang down lower than the narrow end.

Take the broad end in your right hand and move it to the left across the narrower end, which you are holding with your left hand. Now pass the broad end around the narrow end so that it ends up lying on the left. The shape of the necktie knot is now beginning to take shape.

Now pass the broad end underneath the half-formed knot, raising the knot slightly as you do so. Using your left hand, pass the broad end over the knot from underneath and pull the whole of the broad end through to the front. With your right hand, pass the broad end of the necktie between the layer of the knot that is on top and the layer directly beneath it and pull it through. Keeping a firm hold on the narrow end of the necktie, slowly tighten the knot. Finally, press a little "dimple" into the silk fabric just below the knot.

Important: When the knot is finished, the two ends should be more or less the same length and just reach the belt buckle or pants waistband. In the case of tall men, this may not be possible as a necktie averaging just under 5 feet (1.45 m) in length will be too short. If necessary, the broad part of the necktie can hang down to touch the waistband, leaving the narrower side much shorter.

The Prince Albert knot

Smaller men often have problems with long neckties. It may be helpful in their case to wrap the broad end around several times. This style of knot is called a Prince Albert knot. If you prefer an extra large but longish knot, a style which is also very popular with the Italians, this knot is well worth mastering. The method is almost identical to the four-in-hand or simple knot.

Place the necktie around your neck so that the broader end hangs down on the right side. Leave a little extra length on the broader part of the necktie. Taking the broader end in your right hand, pass it over to the left across the narrow end. Now wrap the broad end around the narrow one so that it ends up on the left side again. In contrast to the four-in-hand necktie knot,

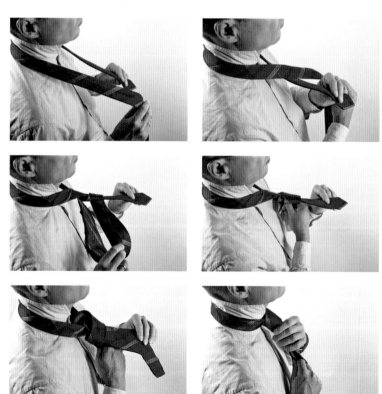

this step is repeated for the Prince Albert knot and the broad end is wrapped around the narrow end a second time, ending once again on the left side. If you prefer a very thick knot, you can repeat this procedure a third time. The final step of the Prince Albert knot is practically identical with the simple knot. Pass the wide end underneath the half-tied knot, lifting it slightly as you do so. With your left hand, pass the wide end from underneath through the half-tied knot and pull the entire wide end all the way through to the front.

With your right hand, pass the broad end through the loop between the top layer and the layers beneath and pull it through. You may not manage to get it right first time without disrupting the various layers. If necessary, start again from the beginning. The final step is to hold onto the narrow end and slowly tighten the knot.

The small knot

The small knot involves fewer wraparounds, thereby using up less material. The necktie also ends up considerably longer as a result. This is consequently a perfect solution for the taller man, as well as for shorter neckties.

This style of knot is also ideal for large-volume types of fabric, such as wool or cashmere. Thicker materials do not end up with such a thick knot because the tie is deliberately not wrapped around so many times.

The small knot differs from the other knots described above in that it starts off in a completely different way. The necktie is placed around the neck with the seam side facing outwards. The wide end should lie on the left side with the narrow end

placed across it. Move the wide end across to the left over the narrow end. Then pass the wide end underneath the narrow end behind the knot and pull it through to the front.

Next, pass the wide end of the necktie over the narrow end and through the loop, pulling it all the way through the half-tied knot.

The knot is finished off in the same way as all other knots—by tightening the knot and pressing a small dimple into the material just beneath the knot. Just as a four-in-hand knot can be expanded into a thicker knot, the small knot can likewise be modified by wrapping the broad end around several times.

Neckties: three ways to make a necktie

There are three ways of making a necktie. The simplest way is to sew the tube of fabric using an ordinary sewing machine. The disadvantage of this is that the seam, consisting of an upper and lower thread, is inflexible, leaving the necktie difficult to tie. The second method uses a special sewing machine called a Liba machine, which uses a single thread and requires the necktie to be turned inside out (and then turned right side out again). The third method consists of sewing a necktie by hand. This involves cutting out the necktie by hand, laying it in the right form, fixing it in shape with pins, and then stitching it together with a needle and thread. The best neckties use the last two methods but the hand-sewn necktie is the cream of the crop.

CUTTING OUT The first step is to flatten the silk out on the table before cutting it out with shears. In the case of single-color products, a whole pile of fabric lengths can be processed at once, using a machine, whereas patterned versions usually require individual attention by hand in order to make sure the pattern aligns correctly in the finished product. Special templates specify the length and width of the individual pieces. These are usually made from trans-

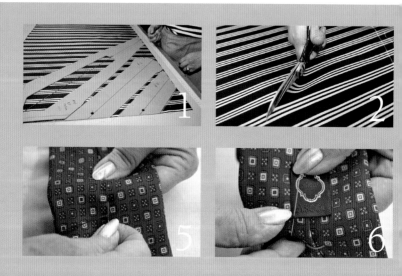

parent plastic so that the cutter can see the fabric design better. Top-quality work is evident at a glance: The pattern is level and runs straight down the middle to the tip of the necktie.

THE INLAY AND LINING The inlay, lining, and the material for the loop on the back of the necktie are prepared at the same time as the outer fabric is cut. The inlay is made of cotton or wool, while the tips of the tie are lined with pure silk, according to the Bemberg method, or with the same material as the necktie itself. The latter process, which experts call "self-tipping," is especially popular in Italy. Whether or not a necktie is easy to tie when it is finished depends largely on whether the inlay is a perfect fit. The inlay should go right up to the edges on the inside of the necktie. If the inlay is too wide, the outer fabric will crease; if it is too narrow, it will slip back and forth.

SEWING A NECKTIE Once the outer fabric, inlay and lining for the tips of the necktie have been placed together, the necktie is sewn together inside out. If a Liba sewing machine is used for this purpose, the necktie is first turned inside out, then turned right way out again after the seam has been closed. Hand-sewn ties must first be laid out in their final shape, fixed together with pins to prevent any shifting during sewing, and then slip-stitched together by hand. A hand-sewn necktie is identifiable from the leftover thread on the inner side of the broad end of the necktie. This thread should never be cut off or the whole necktie might unravel. Finally, the loop of material is sewn onto the back of the narrow end of the necktie and the label added. The final step is to press the necktie carefully to remove any creases.

Ascot, a firm based in Krefeld, Germany, has been making neckties, bow ties, and knitted ties since 1908.

1. Templates, 2. Cutting the fabric, 3. Inlay and lining, 4. Pinning, 5. Sewing, 6. Attaching the label, 7. Ironing and finishing.

The dress handkerchief

A suit or jacket is incomplete without a dress handkerchief. A breast pocket looks empty and neglected without one. Yet many men are reluctant to use this accessory, as they consider it too formal or do not wish to appear dandyish, or find it difficult to fold it into the right shape.

TYPES OF FABRIC Dress handkerchiefs can be made of linen, silk, cashmere, or wool. The most popular options are linen and silk. Cotton is not customary but is nevertheless a common alternative. Beware of handkerchiefs made of shirt fabrics as these are not an elegant option, particularly if the shirt and handkerchief are made of the same material. The result looks unimaginative—and it also appears as if you are showing your shirt front through a hole in your jacket. Linen handkerchiefs are usually white but other colors are also acceptable. A white linen handkerchief is by far the most versatile and most elegant option. It goes with any type of suit or even with a dark-blue blazer.

FINISHING AND SIZE Pocket handkerchiefs in any fabric should be finished with hand-rolled edges in the same way as a high-quality ladies' silk scarf. This should go without saying—machine-hemmed edges simply look cheap and unattractive. It is important that the handkerchief is large enough not to look lost in the breast pocket. It should measure a minimum of 17 inches square (43 x 43 cm) or, ideally, 18.5 inches square (47 x 47 cm). Many handkerchiefs sold in stores are too simple and small, and do not produce enough volume when folded, especially in the breast pocket of a tall, broad-shouldered man.

HOW TO FOLD A HANDKERCHIEF
This often causes confusion, yet is actually quite simple. Making a paper plane is far more difficult. The simplest method is as follows: Fold the handkerchief into a longish rectangle and tuck it into the breast pocket. It can be folded along the lower edge to adjust how much extends above the pocket. The outer corner of the handkerchief should point toward the left shoulder. This type of fold is appropriate for a white linen handkerchief on a formal occasion. Alternatively, take hold of the handkerchief in the middle, loosely grasp the corners with the other hand and tuck it into the pocket so that the ends poke above the pocket, pointing to the left.

With a silk, wool, or cashmere square, take hold of the corners, gently puff up the bottom, then with points facing down, tuck it into the pocket. It is best to forget about more complicated or time-consuming types of folds, which are better suited to starched napkins.

COORDINATING A POCKET HANDKERCHIEF There are some bizarre ideas surrounding the question of how to coordinate a handkerchief with a suit, shirt, or tie. It is actually quite simple and logical. A white linen handkerchief can be worn with any type of day suit (and even with a morning coat, tuxedo or evening dress), and goes with any color of shirt or necktie. Colored handkerchiefs should match the rest of the clothes, with the handkerchief picking up the colors in the necktie. The patterns should not conflict with one another. Neckties with small patterns should be teamed with handkerchiefs with big patterns and vice versa. The shirt color should provide a neutral background for the necktie and handkerchief. For example: dark-blue suit, light-blue shirt, and regimental necktie in wine-red and dark-blue stripes (block stripes) teamed with a Paisley handkerchief in dark red and blue, plus other colors, such as orange.

Folding styles

MASTERING THREE WAYS OF FOLDING A HANDKERCHIEF WILL EQUIP YOU FOR ALL OCCASIONS AND LOOKS.

THE LOOSE FOLD
A severe white linen handkerchief is softened by wearing it in a loose style of fold. This is a familiar sight in Italy worn with a dark business suit in navy or charcoal gray. However, this style of fold makes the pocket bulge considerably.

THE FORMAL FOLD
A traditional, discreet fold is most suitable for formal occasions or to go with a dark suit. For the person opposite you, it will prove less of a distraction from your face, which is why this type of fold is most appropriate for public speaking.

THE POINT STYLE
This type of fold highlights the sheen and structure of a silk or cashmere handkerchief worn with a sports jacket. It can be personalized merely by introducing individual folds.

The basic looks

The dark-gray suit and vest (Cove & Co.) is the most formal option for the office. Depending on your position and field of work, it is appropriate for daily wear or for important meetings or official occasions.

A dark-blue, single-breasted suit (pictured here: a custom-made model by Cove & Co.) should be part of every gentleman's wardrobe. It is indispensable for business and for private occasions. Classic styles endure the longest.

Double-breasted suits always look a little more formal and "dressed up" than single-breasted ones. Contrary to common belief, this model (Cove & Co.) looks good on any figure and is even suitable for the younger man.

Anyone who finds the idea of a double-breasted suit appealing should also try a model with two fastening buttons (Cove & Co.). The longer lapel elongates the upper body and permits more of the necktie and shirt-front to be seen.

The Glen plaid suit (Cove & Co.) was originally considered a sporting outfit by the British and in no way appropriate for office wear. This design is a popular all-rounder not just in the USA but also in continental Europe.

The color of this lightweight cotton suit (Cove & Co.) breaks all the rules but an exception can be made during warm weather. In the USA, this style has long been a summer classic while in Europe it is acceptable on especially hot summer days.

In summer and on less formal occasions, suits may be a little lighter in color (except in the evening). A lighter gray (Cove & Co.) would also be acceptable for business trips, possibly even with a pattern (e.g. fine stripes).

The dark-blue pin-striped suit (Cove & Co.) is regarded in Britain as the uniform of bankers and financiers. In other countries, the stripes would be considered too obtrusive.

Overcoats and jackets

What is the point of an elegant suit if it is hidden beneath an unstylish overcoat? Many men do not believe the protective, outer layer of their outfit is as important as what is underneath. But what if you happen to encounter your business partners in the elevator while your dark suit is still hidden beneath an inappropriate—if useful—raincoat from the outdoor store? If they are wearing similar garments themselves, it will not really matter. Otherwise, it will be embarrassing.

(Left page) The lightweight English quilted jacket was originally designed for riding and shooting activities. Like the waxed jacket, it is often worn in the city over a suit to signal a country lifestyle.

(Above) The covert coat with its contrasting brown or dark-green velvet collar is the favorite of any gentleman fond of English traditions. It is only authentic if it is made from the genuine cloth, e.g. from John G. Hardy fabrics.

The classic overcoat for the office is fashioned from dark cloth. Contrary to business dress code rules on color, however, camel is also an entirely acceptable option (Cove & Co.). Genuine camel hair is exceptionally light and soft. Cashmere is also available in this color.

Lighter in color but nevertheless suitable for business wear is the Chesterfield (Cove & Co.). Typical characteristics are the gray herringbone pattern and the black velvet collar. It goes well with the dark pants of the business suit showing beneath the coat.

You have to be extremely careful with light-colored coats, which is why they project a distinctly luxurious image. They may be made of wool, camel hair, cashmere, or even cotton, and sport a contrasting collar in a different color (Cove & Co.).

Overcoats are not exclusively the domain of the work uniform. Anyone with an eye for classic style may wear a coat over smart casual wear or as part of the "business casual" look. Eccentric linings are a popular way of rounding off the look (Cove & Co.).

A belted cotton gabardine trench coat is the businessman's coat for everyday wear and business trips. The fabric is breathable and relatively waterproof. Shorter coats may be more fashionable but longer ones afford better protection for the suit underneath.

Anyone who dislikes trench coats can opt instead for the so-called "slip-on" raincoat with raglan sleeves. It does just as good a job but is less military in appearance and perhaps rather more elegant. All the leading manufacturers supply both these styles.

The green loden overcoat is particularly associated with Germany or Austria but is no less popular in America and in other parts of Europe. The cloth is light and comparatively waterproof.

The tweed field coat with its built-in waterproof membrane is an elegant outdoor jacket, which has been espoused by many gentlemen as an alternative to the waxed jacket. It is much more pleasant to wear and it keeps you dry without any additional maintenance.

Getting the right fit and alterations

Whether the fit of a suit is merely good or absolutely perfect is something that is often decided by a few millimeters. Anyone who does not wish to leave his appearance to chance should take these millimeters seriously. Whether a garment is too wide, too tight, too long, or too short is not just a question of appearance—a precise fit also determines whether a garment is comfortable to wear. Five millimeters too wide on the waistband and the pants will start to drop down a little even if you merely slip some keys into the pocket. Five millimeters too narrow and the waistband may well become uncomfortably tight after eating. You may not even be consciously aware of such problems but they will often lead to a particular suit being left hanging in

the wardrobe more often than the others. This would be a pity because with just a few simple alterations it could turn into your absolute favorite.

1 It must be your decision whether alterations are necessary and, if so, where. Sales staff seldom give objective advice, as their primary concern is to sell. Start by making sure that the size is right. If you do not know your size, have it measured—US suit sizes are based on chest size in inches, but if buying a suit from Europe you generally need to add 10 to the American size. The pants should be tried on first. They should fit around the waist in such a way that they do not slip down, even without a belt, but not so tightly that they constrict

The length of a suit or sports jacket is dictated by fluctuations in fashion but, generally speaking, the seat should be covered. The length influences the appearance of the figure: shorter length elongates, longer length shortens.

you (so best avoid going shopping on a full stomach). Pants should not be altered by more than one size otherwise the pockets will no longer be in the correct place.

2 The width of the pants leg is extremely important for the overall appearance of the suit, yet few people realize that this is something that can be corrected very easily. Alteration measurements are taken at the hem around the ankle. The lower leg width on a narrow pair of pants without waistband pleats (Size 40) is about 8 inches (20 cm) but on a pleated pair it is 8.5–10 inches (22–25 cm). Tailors carrying out alterations run the tape measure right around the pants leg so the leg width measure is double. Smaller, stockier men would do well to avoid wide-leg pants as they tend to shorten the figure.

3 If the ankle width needs altering, this is best done in conjunction with the whole leg. Top-quality pants are unhemmed when they are sold so that the length can precisely fit the customer's requirements. If you are not sure whether a suit looks better with or without cuffs, begin by ordering cuffs. These can always be removed at a later date. If, on the other hand, a plain leg has been chosen, there will often not be enough fabric in the hem (i.e. where the fabric has been turned up inside the pants leg) to conjure cuffs out of it. Edging tape on the inside of the hem is not necessary and synthetic tape has even been known to cause scratches to shoes.

4 The length of the pants depends on the cut and style. Wider styles are worn longer while narrow pants should be shorter. Wider pants should have a front crease which reaches the top of the instep. The hem at the back should end somewhere between mid-heel and where the heel of the shoe begins. Many outfitters maintain that pants should fall to the middle of the shoe heel but this is too long. Narrow-cut pants are worn shorter. They sit slightly higher at the front and drop .

Wider pants should fall into a single crease across the instep while dropping no lower than the beginning of the shoe heel at the back. Pants are considered "wide" when they cover two thirds of the shoe.

Narrow pants should be worn shorter. They should fall into a gentle crease on the instep and drop no lower than the middle of the heel cap at the back. It is sometimes useful to taper the lower hem of the pants.

Many suit retailers sell sports jackets with sleeves that are far too long. Hence, an extra reminder: The shirt cuff should extend between one quarter and three quarters of an inch (half a centimeter and two centimeters), depending on individual height and taste.

below the edge of the shoe at the back or down to mid-heel. It is often helpful to taper the hem of the pants, making it shorter at the front than at the back.

5 A jacket is only worth altering if the overall length is right. It is considered correct if the seat is covered and the fastening button is on or a bit above the navel. According to the Golden Ratio, this is the body's perfect center. The position of the pockets and buttonholes is determined in relation to the overall length. If this were altered, the resulting position of the pockets and buttons would be too high or too low. The first step is to check the fit of the collar, across the back and shoulders. The collar should fit snugly around the neck. If not, it would be better to choose a different suit since alterations to the collar are a relatively complicated business. A fairly easy problem to correct, on the other hand, is the dreaded crease across

the neck at the back of the jacket. This is where the material below the collar line is pushed upward, causing a horizontal crease. The fabric must lie flat across the back and there should be a small reserve of fabric just behind the arms. Without this, the wearer would not be able to move his arms forward without causing a crease to appear.

6 A jacket must be fastened in order to check whether it is the right width around the waist. The button is then gently pulled away from the body. If this results in a gap of about an inch (two to three centimeters), the waist fit is correct. Any more and the jacket is too wide. This problem can be solved by taking in fabric along the side seams. The waist fit is also a matter of style and comfort. For me, the test is whether the jacket fastens easily yet still feels buttoned up. Many men believe a tailored fit means excessive tightness around the waist. This is complete nonsense. If the jacket strains across

The jacket should not strain across the chest and certainly not pop open when it is fastened. Anyone who is extremely muscular across the chest is unlikely to find a ready-to-wear jacket that fits in this area.

the stomach and the side seams gape open, the garment is simply too tight.

7 Correct sleeve length is essential if the jacket is to look good. If the sleeves reach the wrist, the jacket is too big. If they are too short, the jacket looks too small. For the jacket sleeves to be the correct length, the shirt cuffs must extend a little beyond the sleeve—between one quarter and three quarters of an inch (half a centimeter and two centimeters), depending on taste and height. In the case of a normal, ready-to-wear suit it is a simple matter to shorten or lengthen the sleeves. The tailor will remove the buttons from the sleeve cuff, shorten or lengthen the sleeves, then sew the buttons back on again. In the case of suits with button-up sleeves, this is not possible as the button-holes cannot be repositioned. For this reason, only custom-made jackets have sleeves which really button up.

8 Alterations to the sleeve also involve alterations to the armhole. This is the only correction that no one sees but it is very important. It is necessary when the jacket is too tight under the arms but fits perfectly in all other respects. It should be unnecessary in this instance to resort to another style or contemplate a different size. Nevertheless, the procedure can be quite problematical. The first step is to remove the sleeves and enlarge the two armholes. The sleeves must then be altered to fit the new armholes before being reattached correctly. This task is the exclusive preserve of master tailors, who are well paid for this type of operation.

AN ELEGANT SUIT IS A MARK OF STATURE AND BESTOWS CHARACTER AND STYLE ON THE WEARER.

Formal wear

When I was a child, we still kept what we called a "good pair of pants" for best. These were usually made from grey woolen material and reserved for special occasions. They were only brought out at irregular intervals and were worn with a white shirt and pullover. Many men still keep "an outfit for best" in their wardrobe, but of course for an adult that doesn't mean simply pants. It could be a black suit or sports jacket in a color which is deemed "festive." Only very few men possess a tuxedo, tails, or morning dress.

The conviction that you need to make an extra special effort with your clothing in certain situations is deeply rooted in the human mind. Even someone with no interest at all in fashion realizes that a wedding, for example, is the perfect occasion to wear a suit. But very few people nowadays are interested in any of this. Those who do have an interest in fashion and style are delighted when such occasions come along as they present a welcome opportunity to get dressed up to the nines. This is perhaps especially so when a suit is not your usual working outfit. However, even an office worker, who wears a necktie for work on a daily basis, can still relish the pleasure of wearing a tuxedo or a morning coat. After all, no other outfit can make a man look more elegant.

Tails and morning coats are fashion dinosaurs—their origins date back to the 18th century. They were originally designed for horseback riding, the slit tails hung down to the right and left of the horse's back. The front edges were likewise conceived with the rider in mind, allowing him freedom of movement. In the mid-19th century, tails became accepted daytime wear, along with the frock coat and morning dress. During the early 20th century, the modern suit gradually began to make its appearance. Tails survived as an integral part of evening wear while morning dress was reserved for special daytime occasions and the frock coat disappeared completely from the scene. The tuxedo was a new arrival and regarded as a modern alternative to the evening suit.

Jan-Henrik Scheper-Stuke, the young chief executive at Edsor Kronen, a Berlin-based firm of necktie manufacturers, displays old-school elegance in velvet and silk.

DRESS CODE "Dress code" is a term denoting the rules regarding clothing for a particular event. For example, the dress code may indicate that a necktie and sports jacket are obligatory. Invitations usually state the expected dress code, e.g. "evening dress," or "black tie," etc. Different business sectors can also prescribe what they consider appropriate dress: casinos, for example, can insist on certain dress codes, only admitting men wearing neckties.

BLACK TIE/CRAVATE NOIRE Black tie (or in French *cravate noire*) refers to the black bow tie worn with an evening suit, but also implies the tuxedo itself. In England, the tuxedo is usually referred to as a "dinner jacket," and Germans have traditionally used the term "little society suit." The word originates from the Tuxedo Club on Tuxedo Lake, N.Y.

OCCASIONS REQUIRING A TUXEDO Balls and proms at which tails may not be compulsory, dinner parties (i.e. dinner in elegant surroundings), or sometimes the opera, theater, or a music concert (however this practice is becoming less and less common, although charity premières do still sometimes require it).

The only daytime event at which a tuxedo or dinner jacket would be appropriate is the Glyndebourne opera festival in Sussex (England), which takes place from May to August. Since darkness does not fall until late evening at this time of the year, guests can famously be seen picnicking on the grass in full evening dress.

WHITE TIE/CRAVATE BLANCHE White tie (or *cravate blanche* in French) events tend to be much more formal, requiring full evening dress. Soldiers are permitted to wear dress uniform. At international events, national costume is also permitted. Men and women alike are also permitted to wear medals and orders.

FORMAL OCCASIONS DEMANDING FULL EVENING DRESS Opera balls, Nobel Prize ceremonies, state banquets and dinners, balls to celebrate aristocratic weddings.

MORNING DRESS OR CUTAWAY COAT Morning dress is the most formal type of daytime suit. It was similar to a frock coat, only with a cutaway front, giving it the alternative name "cutaway," sometimes shortened to "cut." It was the British who called it a "morning coat," accurately alluding to the time of day when it should be worn.

The morning coat's angular front panels are cut in such a way as to allow the wearer more freedom of movement than with the frock coat.

OCCASIONS DEMANDING MORNING DRESS Traditional aristocratic weddings, state funerals, state receptions, the Queen's garden parties, Investiture ceremonies.

special occasions

THE DARK SUIT The dark suit is an all-round outfit suitable for just about any special daytime or evening occasion. It can be worn at all times unless the invitation states otherwise.

The dark suit includes a single- or double-breasted suit (or a suit and vest) in dark gray or blue (not black), complemented with white shirt (or pale blue or pink for daytime wear), a discreetly patterned necktie, and black shoes.

COME AS YOU ARE This is a familiar instruction in the English-speaking world. It does not, however, suggest that you should jump up from the sofa and arrive at a party or private exhibition viewing wearing your leisure gear. What it does mean is that you can turn up straight from the office without changing into evening wear. Men should wear a suit and tie, women a pantsuit or skirt and jacket, or an elegant smart casual outfit.

COME-AS-YOU-ARE OCCASIONS Private exhibition viewings, book launches, fashion shows, poetry readings, lectures, club evenings, and parties.

If the occasion demands a tuxedo or tails, these must be teamed with the appropriate shoe—in black, patent leather.

Morning dress

Morning dress comes in a range of colors and fabrics but the traditional, classic colors are still the most popular: black cutaway coat, light gray vest, striped pants, black Oxfords, white shirt with turn-down collar and double cuffs, necktie and, the crowning glory, a black top hat.

One of the most common alternatives to this traditional version is light gray morning dress (i.e. cutaway coat with vest and pants to match). This may be worn at weddings, but only by the groom and his best man, or for race meetings at Ascot. Both traditions originate in English-speaking countries so the dress code governing them is not universally applicable. Morning dress also comes in charcoal gray, a version which is considered extremely versatile. This option consists of a coat, pants, and vest all in the same color, but it is a less common alternative. Pants worn with morning dress may be striped, or in Shepherd's or Glen plaid. There are numerous variations of the basic vest: For funerals, the vest should generally be in black. For all other morning dress occasions of a happier nature, lighter shades are usually the norm. British men often opt for a "buff-colored" vest, a sort of cream or beige color. Linen is also acceptable for the summer. For the rest of the year, vests with imaginative patterns are also popular. Tastes differ considerably in this respect, but in men's fashion there is a tradition of choosing a vest in a luxury or elaborately embroidered fabric.

The Stresemann, or stroller suit, is a semi-formal outfit which may sometimes be worn as a counterpart to morning dress. However, it is not entirely appropriate. The Stresemann suit was an invention from the period following the First World War and was originally designed for office wear. In the case of a Stresemann, the morning coat is replaced by a black jacket, while the rest is based on the morning dress. Since occasions requiring morning dress are generally held by tradition-conscious hosts, a Stresemann would, generally speaking, be inappropriate. Today the name "Stresemann" is only used in German-speaking countries (and is sometimes called a "Bonn suit"), however it is unknown in other countries and consequently does not usually feature in the dress code.

Standard morning dress with a gray vest, white shirt, and striped pants. (All photos: Cove & Co.)

In summer, linen vests—in pastel shades, if so desired— are an excellent choice to wear with a morning coat.

British men and Anglophiles tend to favor a "buff" or cream-colored vest, an option which is always an acceptable alternative to gray. Only funerals require a black vest to be worn.

The tuxedo

A tuxedo is a black evening jacket with silk facing on the lapels and a plain silk stripe, or braid, on the pants along the outside leg seam, and is worn with a white evening shirt, black bow tie, dress handkerchief (white linen or colored silk), black silk knee socks (or fine woolen ones) and evening lace-up shoes or pumps with a corded silk (grosgrain) bow. Although the tuxedo may be considered very formal by some people, it dates back no further than the period between the end of the 19th century and the First World War, having originally been introduced as a comfortable alternative to full evening dress, or tails, from which it took its color and—in

An evening suit sometimes comprises a light-colored jacket (right in the photo). This style of tuxedo is worn at sea or at open-air venues, but only ever in the evening.

its original version—the vest (admittedly in black). Essentially, however, the tuxedo is closely related to the street suit.

Several versions of this style are available: either single-breasted, with or without a vest, or double-breasted, with a shawl collar or peaked lapels. If you order a custom-made tuxedo, you can create a fairly individual design, whereas with ready-to-wear, the choice is usually limited to just two types of lapel and between single- and double-breasted styles.

There is only one alternative to black, namely the shade known as "midnight blue." This was allegedly invented by the Prince of Wales (who later became the Duke of Windsor) because the usual black had a greenish tinge under artificial lighting.

Although I, personally, have never noticed this, deep blue is certainly an attractive alternative. However, the lapels and braids on the pants should still be black. A nice touch would be a velvet collar or silk-faced sleeve cuffs, features which would virtually never be found in ready-to-wear tuxedos.

A black bow tie is obligatory, any other color being wrong. Anyone who wants to break with this tradition must have a good sense of style (in which case the result might well turn out OK).

The long necktie, which in the past was often worn with a tuxedo, now seems largely out of place. If you prefer not to wear a bow tie, you can simply wear a black suit with a black tie in the evening instead of a tuxedo.

The velvet smoking jacket

MORE THAN JUST COUNTRY ATTIRE FOR CIGAR SMOKERS AND OTHER BON VIVEURS.

The British name for the tuxedo is a "dinner jacket": In other countries, in other languages, this type of jacket is sometimes referred to as a "Smoking." This is misleading, as a "smoking jacket" is a velvet evening jacket invented to enhance the enjoyment of tobacco. During the late 19th century, after dinner with the ladies, gentlemen used to don smoking jackets and withdraw to a special room to smoke tobacco. When they

returned in their original jackets, no whiff of tobacco fumes from the smoke-impregnated jacket could cause offence.

Since modern-day smokers are once again obliged to occupy separate rooms, the smoking jacket may soon experience a revival. Until then, it will continue to serve as an alternative to the normal dinner suit, in which case it simply replaces the suit jacket. Embroidered velvet slippers—matching the jacket, naturally—should be worn on the feet.

Evening dress or tails

Tails have formed part of a gentleman's wardrobe longer than any other item of clothing. They have remained relatively unchanged since the 18th century. Long pants are a much more recent element, as the tailcoat was originally worn with knee-breeches. This type of outfit was originally designed for horseback riding, hence the angled points on the front panels to allow the legs more freedom of movement.

The bow tie worn with tails is always made in white cotton piqué. In addition, the dress shirt must have a wing collar, cuffs, and front made of the same material, full evening-dress pants with silk stripes, and evening shoes (pumps with a corded silk bow).

The stand-up collar is obligatory with tails. To be precise, this should be a starched wing collar. For a really formal look, it should be very stiff and cover a large amount of neck. Button-down shirts are naturally softer to wear but if tails are the order of the day, the wearer will simply have to put up with some discomfort. A stiff, high collar will encourage a man to hold himself proudly and upright. If you are wearing tails, you cannot simply pull any old dress shirt out from the wardrobe, as this will have a different type of cuff. The appropriate shirt to wear with tails has single cuffs, which fasten with cuff links. The dress shirt required for a tuxedo should have double or French cuffs, similar to a suit shirt.

Since the days of Fred Astaire, tailors have been debating how tails should be cut and whether or not the vest should show below the dress-coat front. It must be borne in mind, in this respect, that in the Thirties, the waistband was expected to sit on the waist, which meant that the vest could also be high. Even today, pants tailored in this style are still considered elegant, although many men now prefer pants which sit lower on the waist. The vest then slips down and inevitably shows beneath the lower edge of the tailcoat. This has the effect of shifting the optical center of the body downward, thus dividing the figure into two unflattering halves.

A cape would provide the finishing touch for anyone who enjoys a touch of the theatrical.

*Top hat and tails are
a proverbial twosome.
However, the tall hat should
only ever be worn outdoors
and immediately removed
upon entering a building.*

The bow tie

The most formal type of necktie is the bow tie. A white bow tie (made from cotton piqué) is worn with tails while a black, silk bow tie is reserved for the tuxedo. This is a hard-and-fast rule for tails but alternatives are permitted to the black tuxedo bow tie.

Some men may opt for a patterned tie: The discreet option would be tiny, white polka dots on a black background, whereas other color combinations would be more daring. During the Seventies, velvet bow ties were also a popular accessory to wear with a tuxedo, e.g. in wine red or purple. Bottle green is another excellent alternative. However, if in doubt, black is still the best choice. And please, never wear a white bow tie with a tuxedo.

Either way, they should both be hand-tied. In the case of the necktie, this is self-evident even to non-fashionistas.

Fortunately, pre-tied, clip-on neckties have virtually died out. In the case of the bow tie, however, even the most stylish and quality-conscious gentlemen are not averse to clipping a convenience bow tie around their neck. And yet it is so easy to tie a bow

tie that even a child could do it—at least the sort of child who can tie his or her own shoelaces.

A bow is just a bow, after all, regardless of whether it is tied around the neck or on one's shoe. The first attempt may not always be successful, but if you allow yourself sufficient time, you should be able to get it right, even if it is your first attempt.

An alternative to the tuxedo

The tuxedo is the outfit with a James Bond image. It makes a man feel elegant, self-assured and cool. Nonetheless, there are numerous men who do not wear tuxedos. There are many reasons for this—it is often a matter of economy and concerns over whether it would get enough wear. In my experience, if you purchase a tuxedo, special occasions often follow. However, anyone who cannot drum up enough enthusiasm for a tuxedo can still dress well for the evening.

THE BLACK SUIT Sixty years ago, virtually every man owned a black suit. Not a tuxedo, admittedly, but a black street suit. It was brought out of the wardrobe for church visits, for christenings, weddings, and, of course, funerals. And in the evening, it also served as a good suit for dining in a restaurant, drinking cocktails, or going to the theater. The black suit disappeared from the scene during the Seventies and Eighties, before re-emerging toward the end of the Nineties as a symbol of designer chic—admittedly as a daytime suit. As far as the dress code is concerned, this is rather absurd since black, as a man's color, is reserved for the evening—or for funerals. This color is not suitable for business wear (apart from shoes). The revival of the black suit has recently given rise to a new culture in evening dress. It is becoming increasingly common in the evening to see fashionably dressed men attired in black suits, sporting a white, open-necked shirt, and perhaps a black necktie. I call it the Tom Ford look. It is chic, modern, but also, elegant. And from here it is only a small step to the tuxedo.

VELVET AND CORD In the 18th century, velvet and silk were commonly used for men's clothing. In the 19th century, they were then largely replaced by wool, a more practical material, and were thereafter only used for neckties, vests, and dress handkerchiefs—and then only as part of evening dress. For this reason, designers are constantly using these fabrics in jackets or entire suits—dandyish outfits, which are suitable, at best, for glamorous nights out. Black is the most suitable color, in this respect, but purple, blue, and wine red are also popular. The quality of velvet depends on the fiber. The best kind of velvet is silk velvet, although it is more commonly produced from cotton.

Corduroy fabrics are closely related to velvet, feel similar to the touch, and are consequently acceptable evening wear despite their simple origins. A black, or dark-blue, fine cord suit would be an excellent evening choice for a youngish, stylish gentleman.

SUIT AND BLAZER A blue suit is really a daytime suit but is also a good choice for the evening. Teamed with a white shirt and dark-blue necktie, the suit looks almost as dressed-up as a tuxedo yet still maintains the look of a going-out uniform. Alternatively, a black necktie (possibly made from black, knitted silk) may be brought into service.

In his book *The Englishman's Suit*, Hardy Amies, tailor and designer to Her Majesty the Queen, suggested the idea of teaming a dark-blue blazer with pants made of the same material and combining these with a black bow tie. This elegant combination was also found in the wardrobe of the late Duke of Windsor—a set of brass buttons completed the uniform style of the jacket.

Wedding suits

Weddings provide one of the few opportunities for men to don a suit or to dress formally in some other style. Although some distinction is normally made, depending on whether you are the groom, bride's father, or a guest, the dress code for weddings is fairly clear on the outfit for each of the roles.

The most frequently quoted rule of thumb is that a guest should not turn up dressed more elegantly than the bridal pair. However, if the latter opt for a particularly eccentric style of dress which is far outside the usual fashion norms—because they are Heavy Metal fans, for example, and wish to make a feature of this at their wedding, then the guest will find himself facing a dilemma: whether to conform to this theme or not. In such circumstances, it would be wise to check in advance exactly how the hosts feel about the celebrations marking their wedding.

If the above-mentioned Heavy Metal wedding couple regard their own outfits of Slayer T-shirt and leather vest as festive, the guest has no need to don fancy dress but can turn up in whatever clothing he considers appropriate for the occasion. If the bridal pair themselves are not concerned about dress codes, then even a casual outfit would be in order. No matter how important it is to respect the standards of the host, no one should have to jump through hoops to fit in. Far better not to accept the invitation in the first place.

CIVIL WEDDINGS Civil weddings were traditionally nothing more than an administrative procedure, carried out in normal or formal day wear. Gentlemen (the bridegroom and guests) wore dark suits, though lighter-colored ones were acceptable in summer. These same rules can still apply today: Dressing up in formal clothes was always reserved for church weddings. But nowadays, since church nuptials are often dispensed with, many couples treat a civil wedding as they would a church ceremony, extending the occasion to include unctuous speeches by the presiding official, a white dress, and bridesmaids. Given this type of situation, any clothing suitable for a church ceremony would also be suitable here—even though this is not how it was originally meant to be.

CHURCH As a rule, church weddings are held during the daytime and the groom and male guests wear formal day suits. The most formal option is morning dress (cf. p. 67) but a dark suit may also be worn. It is customary in some countries to wear a tuxedo for church weddings, but this is not technically correct. Tuxedos should only be worn as evening wear.

In the case of summer weddings or country weddings, a lighter-colored or even a casual suit may be worn instead of the dark suit but this does not look very dressed up. Gold satin morning coats and embroidered vests are also enjoying considerable popularity at present but such garments are not really very tasteful.

Some couples want their wedding to reflect their personal tastes or celebrate their hobbies, in which case they may appear dressed as a cowboy and cowgirl, wearing Goth outfits, or dressed in historical costumes. Some guests might find such spectacles amusing while others would simply find them embarrassing. However, tolerance is the key in this respect.

WEDDING RECEPTION This usually takes place straight after the ceremony, leaving no time to change. The clothes chosen for the wedding ceremony will, therefore, also be worn for the reception.

EVENING WEDDING RECEPTION It is up to the hosts to decide how formal they want their evening celebrations to be. Another factor to consider is what people have been wearing throughout the day and whether there will be time enough for a change of outfit.

For example, anyone who has attended the church ceremony during the day wearing a morning coat will inevitably have to get changed for the evening event. The outfit of choice would be a tuxedo or even tails. Morning dress would never be worn in the evening. Anyone who has opted for a dark suit may keep this on during the evening. Black shoes are essential in this respect.

The boutonniere

MORE THAN ANY OTHER ACCESSORY, THE BOUTONNIERE SINGLES OUT THE ELEGANT GENTLEMAN OF STYLE.

When the bride orders her bouquet from the florist's, she will often order a boutonniere for the groom at the same time. This is fine except for the fact that many men face the problem of having no proper buttonhole on the lapel of their suit jacket. So what to do with the flower? Florists recommend wrapping the stems of a mini flower arrangement in a tiny paper cone which can then be pinned to the suit lapel. However, such advice is naturally guaranteed to make a style-conscious gentleman's

blood run cold, since a suit should be adorned with a flower which is inserted through a hand-sewn buttonhole, not one that is pinned to the lapel. There is, however, no need to rush out and buy a hand-sewn suit with a buttonhole and loop behind the lapel to hold the flower stem. All you need to do is get a gentleman's tailor to cut a buttonhole into the lapel and hem it properly. This will cost a few dollars but will be well worth the expense.

HOW TO ACHIEVE THAT SMART LEISURE LOOK: BEING CASUAL, BUT NOT SLOPPY.

Cool and casual

Most women would agree that men look better in a suit than in an old sweatshirt. However, this does not mean that a man has to wear a suit in order to look good. A smart, casual look can come across as very sexy as well as confident—provided it is not a hotchpotch of leisure garments randomly thrown together, but a carefully chosen outfit from individual items which complement each other to good effect.

First of all, we should consider what is meant by "casual." In some people's opinions, "casual" is a synonym for "sloppy" but this does not have to be the case. However, many men are guilty of precisely this mistake, believing that it does not matter in the slightest what they wear at home in the evening, or on the weekend. All that matters is that it is practical and comfortable. Unfortunately, these two adjectives often preclude the possibility of an outfit looking good, let alone attractive, cool, or self-assured.

It is important, therefore, to show a degree of good taste when it comes to choosing the clothes you wear in your private life. Clothes should reflect a person's role in life. It would be simply ridiculous for a businessman, who is responsible for thousands of employees, to go around outside the office wearing the same sort of clothes he wore as a student or schoolboy. Casual wear should be appropriate to a person's age. It may be okay for an 8-year-old boy to let mom choose his clothes for him, but it would be inappropriate for a 38-year-old man.

Nowadays, the range of different casual looks is greater than ever before and there is something to suit every pocket. During our spare time, we are all free to become the person we cannot be if we are wearing a suit. Clothes give people the chance to express their true self, the alter ego who remains hidden at work beneath the grey twill. Leather jacket, jeans, and boots, a polo shirt and boat shoes—or even a cashmere sweater and corduroy pants, or rugby shirt and chinos.

The sports jacket has been absent from the fashion scene for a long time but is now resuming its rightful place as the indispensable nucleus of a smart-casual wardrobe.

Jeans

Changes in people's thinking are clearly reflected in clothing. Take jeans, for example: At the end of the 19th century, these were work trousers worn by gold prospectors and farm workers. Nowadays, they are cheap everyday wear for men, women, and children, or else coveted designer products for fashion fanatics. How this change came about is outlined below.

It was during the early 20th century that jeans evolved into casual wear for the whole family. In the 1960s, they became the trademark of rebellious youngsters and, in the 1970s, designer jeans became the "in" thing. By the 1980s, they had become socially acceptable. The popularity of jeans dwindled during the 1990s, only to re-emerge later on with an even stronger following than before. What will happen next is anybody's guess.

Jeans are made from a material called denim. Legend has it that the name is derived from a corruption of the French term *serge de Nîmes*, in other words, "cloth from Nîmes." Serge is a twill weave, easily recognizable even to a layman from the

The king of jeans: dark blue.

Smart casual jeans: slightly faded.

diagonal structure of the weave. Another example of a twill weave, familiarly used for trench coats, is gabardine. The diagonal structure is clearly visible on the lighter-colored inside of the material. The fact that jeans are dark on the outside but not on the inside is due to the two colors of thread used in the warp and weft. In denim, the warp thread is dark blue while the weft is white. Together, these threads produce the characteristic jeans look.

What is also interesting is how much the value of the fabric has altered. Whereas jeans were originally cheap and universally affordable, the most expensive versions nowadays are in fact those which most faithfully reflect the early designs.

Authentic jeans, the fabric for which has been produced by old looms, have become cult objects. Collectors also pay high prices for ancient pairs of jeans, which have been lurking in storerooms or hidden away at the back of closets for decades and have turned up in an auction.

THE RIGHT WAY TO WEAR JEANS

When the first dedicated jeans outlets began to appear during the Sixties and Seventies, often the usual sort of specialized sales staff encountered in other clothes stores were replaced by young women, many of whom resembled the kind of dancers you might have seen on a TV pop music show. At least many people believed that was the

Only for leisurewear: washed-out light blue.

For a smarter leisure look: washed-out dark blue.

case. Nowadays, jeans can be bought in every fashion store, and discount stores and supermarkets sell blue jeans, as a matter of course, alongside washing powder and potatoes. The number of jeans wearers has meanwhile mushroomed to such an extent that selling jeans makes sense for just about every retailer.

The basic style of jeans reflects the tried-and-true brands sold by

the original US producers. Dark-blue, straight-cut, relatively high-waisted jeans are equally acceptable as a feature of the classic English style, or the preppy look, teamed with a robust leather flying jacket, tweed peaked cap, and sturdy working boots. Since the Eighties, it has been acceptable for jeans to be worn with a good sports jacket, shirt (without a necktie), and welt-stitched, lace-up shoes for smart leisure occasions or business casual. An important point to remember in this respect is not to choose a belt that is too wide. A perfect choice would be a belt made of English saddle leather with a brass buckle. Fans of horsehide may decide to opt for a belt of cordovan leather.

Anyone with an essentially conservative taste in fashion but who is still quite style-conscious is perfectly at liberty to opt for a slightly trendier style of jeans. A dark fabric (always blue, never black) is de rigueur in this respect, but the jeans can be tighter-fitting, or whatever else current trends dictate. For example, you might choose pants which are slightly flared or sit a bit lower on the waist. Teamed with a shirt, pullover, or sports jacket, the overall outfit will look timeless and not at all outdated.

Jeans, which reflect the fashions of the 1920s to the 1950s, or which copy earlier, original styles down to the last detail, have less appeal for fans of the classic look. They are too closely associated with the early days of jeans when they were still predominantly work trousers or worn by motorcycle gangs and beatniks. Consequently, this original jeans style is mainly favored by people whose clothes sense is still rooted in this sort of fashion scene, i.e. rockabilly fans, or people with similar style tastes, who prefer robustly masculine, traditionally American basics, such as plaid flannel shirts, leather jackets, working boots, and white T-shirts. Highly trendy styles, e.g. skin-tight versions, can look fantastic, reflecting the preppy look or exuding a nerdy irony—but only when worn by very slim youngsters rather than grown men.

White jeans are an exception in this respect and technically not jeans at all. But since they are identical in design to blue jeans, they deserve a mention. They are worn in much the same way as chinos but a tighter fit and horizontal pockets give them a more sporty appearance and make the wearer's legs look slimmer.

The combination of a classic sports jacket, preferably of tweed material, and a pair of dark-blue US jeans is a traditional classic in continental European countries. To this day, this is more commonly seen in Paris, Milan, or Munich than in London or New York.

In their quest for authentic-looking garments, designers and fashionistas have rediscovered traditional-style jackets. Paired with jeans, they create a perfect smart-casual look, which is a successful combination of traditional and casual.

Cool and casual | 85

Chinos

Where would men's fashion be without chinos? Chinos are light-colored cotton pants which allegedly get their name from the fact that they came from China. Whether this was indeed the case when chinos first became popular in America, after the end of the Second World War, remains uncertain. Certainly, most chinos are produced in the US today. Many other Asian countries now also supply the vast US pants market, which continues to be dominated by light, cotton chinos—a type of pants which blend perfectly with the casual yet classic approach to the dress code which now prevails.

Chinos did not become really popular in Europe until the 1980s, even though light-colored pants date back a long way in European fashion history. Even as far back as the 18th century, it was commonplace for men to wear light-colored linen pants, as these could be washed and bleached without difficulty (simply by leaving them in the sun to dry). In the early 19th century in the wake of industrialization, linen began to be replaced by cotton, which was becoming more widely available and was much cheaper in price, which led, in turn, to a surge in the popularity of light cotton pants. The

main feature that these predecessors of chinos have in common with genuine 1940s-style American chinos is color. They look best teamed with dark blue, a combination which was already popular in 18th-century Europe and still works well now.

Chinos were traditionally worn as part of the college look. At a more formal level this means chinos combined with a blazer or sports jacket. Alternatively, a smart-casual look might consist of chinos worn with a shirt and pullover, or short, blouson-style jacket. The most casual option would be chinos teamed with a polo or rugby shirt. The above combinations obviously differ with the season, as do the appropriate shoes, jackets, and coats, and other accessories. Chinos have meanwhile also been adopted as part of the classic British gentleman's look, as well as being an accepted feature of Italian casual style. The question of which style of pants goes with which look, is largely dependent on the cut of the pants. As a rule, the Italians prefer a body-hugging fit, while the British and Americans prefer a more generous cut, often including pleats and cuffs. An eccentric but by no means outlandish alternative is chinos with adjustable side loops, a rear belt, or even buttons for suspenders.

A long-sleeved polo shirt worn over a striped shirt creates a casual look. Worn with chinos, the combination is still essentially chic.

A timeless American classic: light-blue, button-down shirt, navy-blue blazer, and chinos. The addition of shoes, necktie, and sleeveless top can create a variety of different outfits.

Shorts

Many style experts would ideally like to banish short pants as city wear and only permit them on the beach. And rightly so. For a long time, shorts were exclusively children's wear, and grown men in shorts cannot really be taken seriously. What is more, shorts exhibit far more leg than anyone wants to see. They also draw attention to your socks and shoes, which are very prominently on view on the end of a naked leg. And, finally, those opposed to shorts are constantly citing the dress code, which does not sanction the wearing of shorts in towns. All this may very well be correct but the subject can also be viewed in a completely different light.

Individual items of clothing are rarely unattractive or style-less in themselves; more often than not problems arise as a result of the fact that clothes are worn by the wrong people, at the wrong time, and in the wrong place. Bathing thongs may be fine to wear at the swimming pool but not as footwear to wear with a suit. Shorts

Plaid shorts suggest golf or board sports.

Khaki shorts, the all-round classic.

Cargo shorts in olive for an outdoor look.

Dark blue: indispensible for the summer.

are okay given the appropriate weather, surroundings, occasion, age, and figure. The most difficult factors to determine in terms of propriety are age and figure. Some well-toned 70-year-olds look fine wearing shorts on their bicycles but there are also many pudgy 30-year-olds who ought not to be seen in shorts. As far as surroundings are concerned, we are much more tolerant these days. Shorts are now completely acceptable in an urban lakeside café for an evening sundowner, but perhaps not quite as appropriate for a visit to a museum.

The word "shorts" is an abbreviation of "short pants." At one point in his diaries, the author Thomas Mann mentions "short pants" but it is clear from the context that he is referring to knickerbockers. Nowadays, this particular misunderstanding would not arise but there is one which does still occur: namely, that the length of the shorts is a matter of personal taste. Shorts should, at the very least, reach mid-thigh. This minimum length only applies to smaller men for whom this length is ideal in relation to their body height. In the case of taller men, the hem of the shorts should almost reach their knees, without covering them. On no account should the shorts reach down to the calves.

Pack your swimming trunks

WHAT WE WEAR IN WATER REVEALS MORE ABOUT US THAN WE MIGHT THINK.

Swimwear is one area of fashion which is less frequently in the spotlight. Nonetheless, what we wear to go swimming says a good deal about us. It begins with the basic question of whether we wear trunks or shorts for swimming—the length and fit of these reveal a good deal about the true or desired age of the wearer. The younger the wearer, the wider and longer are the shorts. The swim brief is a mini version of swim trunks while the most extreme and style-less option is the swim tanga. A man looks his best in swimming shorts, which are cut like boxers. When traveling, you should bear in mind that in some countries swim briefs are not accepted as giving adequate cover for swimming. It is best to find out before a trip exactly what is appropriate. You should also take into account that while swim briefs may be okay for swimming, they are not acceptable for wandering along the beach promenade. Swimming shorts, which stop just above the knee, are acceptable virtually anywhere, which is why they are the safest style of swimwear to take along to a pool or bathing beach.

The T-shirt

For some people, the T-shirt is nothing more than an undershirt while for others, it is the most versatile garment of all time and a legend of modern fashion. Factually speaking, it was originally an undergarment, but during the 1960s, this simple, cotton top evolved into an important part of the protest outfit worn by all hippies in order to express freedom and individuality. These days, many men still view the T-shirt primarily as an undershirt or even a so-called "basic."

Since the T-shirt was always considered to be a piece of underwear right from the

beginning, there is no dress code to regulate its wear. The recurring question of whether a man may wear a T-shirt with a suit instead of a proper shirt is difficult to answer. But one way of deciding it, is to say that a banker should not wear a T-shirt with his suit, while someone visiting a night club may do so with impunity. How we view this combination is another matter. Fashion sometimes favors it and sometimes not; it is virtually impossible to find a definitive, objective answer to this question. A highly toned model would undoubtedly cut an excellent figure in a T-shirt and suit, whereas a man with a prominent belly would be better off wearing a shirt.

Another frequently asked question is whether it is acceptable for a white T-shirt to be visible beneath an open shirt collar. If the T-shirt is regarded as underwear, then decidedly not. T-shirt fans could choose a V-necked version.

The polo shirt

Despite the many fashion trends that come and go and the very small repertoire of garments and colors which actually comprise a man's wardrobe, there is nevertheless an astonishingly wide range of possibilities for giving expression to your personal taste. However, formal wear, for example, requires that a suit must be teamed with a shirt. Apart from a few variations in detail, there is no real alternative to this. A shirt is, quite simply, the only garment which goes with a dark suit. The range of possibilities in the casual sector is similarly restricted since, apart from the sports shirt, the only other options are the polo shirt and its long-armed cousin, the rugby

shirt. The T-shirt, due to its lack of a collar, is assigned to a different wardrobe category, e.g. athletic clothing or a specific fashion look.

The collar is the key feature. Golf players realized this a long time ago. On the green and in the clubhouse, the dress code prescribes the wearing of shirts. T-shirts are not acceptable. Polo shirts—either short- or long-sleeved—are permitted. This rule can also be applied beyond the golf course. For a start, shirts without collars resemble underwear and do not frame the wearer's face. The collar naturally only frames the lower half of a person's face but means that the neck also looks smarter and is shown in a more flattering light. This becomes increasingly important the older the neck and face are. The importance of polo and rugby shirts is therefore only indirectly connected with the once exclusive nature of the two sports, and the sports' participants for whom the garments were originally developed.

Sweatshirts

A sportswear classic, the sweatshirt also originated in the USA, and its name is a clue to its original purpose: It was worn by athletes during training. The term "sweatshirt" became common in the 1920s when it was first invented. At the time, athletes wore woolen training clothes, and then someone hit upon the brilliant idea of using cotton jersey which, until then, had only been used to make underwear.

Baseball players were the first to be kitted out with sweatshirts, followed soon after, by athletes in many other kinds of sports. Colleges also began to equip their teams with sweatshirts and obviously added their logos or names as well. Since the 1950s, sweatshirts have become a universally accepted type of leisurewear, although they did not really make an impact in Europe until the 1980s.

The hooded sweatshirt, or hoodie, is a variation of the original sweatshirt and appeared just a few years later on. The hood and pockets were a logical addition for sportsmen and sportswomen. In many other respects, the material and basic design are the same for all models. However, the image of the "hoodie" is not always a pleasant one. Many hoodie wearers do not do so to cool down after a run but to maintain their anonymity whilst carrying out criminal acts. Indeed in some countries, the debate surrounding this aspect of the hooded sweatshirt was so vigorous that it even culminated in attempts to get the garment banned. On the other hand, this type of sweatshirt has been a feature of expensive sportswear collections for many years and for many people is a perfectly inoffensive leisurewear garment.

Summer looks

Socks worn with sandals, pasty-white legs in shorts, thongs in the theater—summertime is rife with fashion mistakes. As soon as temperatures begin to rise, male members of the human race lose their inhibitions and begin to discard clothing. Each year, this acts as a signal for articles to start popping up in Italian newspapers, criticizing and ridiculing the sense of style of other races. What is the point of such criticism, however, when models are parading up and down the runway wearing coarsely knitted woolen socks and Jesus sandals? What is wrong with Birkenstocks if Hollywood stars and sex symbols are not ashamed to be seen wearing them? Is it now really the case that "anything goes"?

The most important rule for the summer months is that you must only exhibit the parts of your body that are presentable. This naturally presupposes that a person is capable of exercising a degree of self-criticism—a rare quality. Anyone who feels indignant about flabby stomachs, neglected feet, or unattractive legs should not inflict his own beer belly or the calloused skin of his heels on other people. Rule No. 2: anything goes, but not always. Shorts, for example, are considered fine nowadays for shopping trips in town or for a barbecue—but they are not acceptable for a Golden Wedding celebration or an elegant restaurant. The same applies in the case of sandals and thongs. No one will raise their eyebrows if men or women bare their feet, but such behavior remains unacceptable in a business setting. As for combining socks with sandals: The basic rule is that socks should only be worn with long pants and sandals only with shorts. So logically, open-toed footwear should not come into contact with a sock. Anyone who does not like wearing sandals on bare skin should forego wearing shorts.

It is a big mistake to think that removing one's clothes will bring relief in hot weather. And the city is certainly not the beach. Consequently, in summer a man always looks best in smart leisurewear.

(Left page) Committed sandal wearers are unlikely to switch to lightweight, slip-on shoes no matter how elegant they look. And a fresh-looking, plaid shirt is better suited to a shopping trip than a T-shirt.

Jackets and windbreakers

Anyone who wears a suit or sports jacket all day long to the office probably enjoys wearing something different in his free time. There are many different types of jacket which are extremely popular. In recent years, the padded parka has found particular favor. Given the global warning situation, this is rather surprising. Presumably, it is being bought and worn by city dwellers for the same reason that they buy 4-wheel drive vehicles. The classic, short jacket is the windbreaker, also known as the lumber jacket by the older generation. Underestimated, but no less attractive for all that, are the different styles of safari jackets. Not only do these look slightly more elegant because of their extra length but they also exude an air of authority as the style is reminiscent of a uniform. And, above all, they have lots of pockets.

A light, quilted jacket is an indispensable feature of the preppy look. Those made from 100% synthetic material are the most practical, as they are washable.

(Left page) Short, windbreaker-style jackets have been a staple part of a man's wardrobe since the 1920s. Their silhouette alternates constantly between slim-fitting and blouson-style.

Quilted vests do not look good on everyone but they are a good solution for seasonal transition periods. They also allow more freedom of movement than jackets with sleeves, and so are excellent for those people doing physical work outdoors.

The safari jacket is the perfect leisure look for a gentleman: longer than the windbreaker-style jacket, more casual than a sports jacket, and with lots of pockets.

The field jacket is very similar to the safari jacket. The blue model shown here is better suited to town wear.

Zippered anorak-style jackets are not acceptable as business attire but they are ideal for a sporty, casual look.

Despite global warming, the quilted, down jacket is still very popular, both as a warm basic wardrobe item and as a status symbol.

The parka, a longer version of the quilted jacket, gives protection right down to the knees—a very agreeable feature in really icy weather.

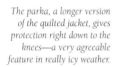

A bomber jacket teamed with chinos, polo shirt, and boat shoes or penny loafers creates a classic American casual look.

Leather jackets

Leather jackets fall into the same category as pipe-smoking or growing a beard. Nearly every man has tried them at some point or at least dreamed of doing so. Those who have plucked up the necessary courage either stick at it or not. And, for many leather jacket enthusiasts, they become something of a trademark. But it often proves difficult for the conservatively dressed gentleman to know how to integrate a leather jacket into his wardrobe.

Leather jackets might not initially seem like a basic item in a gentleman's wardrobe, who is generally far more at home in a sports jacket and sweater, waxed jacket, trench coat, or duffel coat. It does not take long to realize, however, that the leather jacket is also perfectly acceptable for more elegant occasions. We need only recall the classic Italian suede-leather, blouson-style jacket with knitted collar and waistband—

a classic of the smart, casual look. As is the lambs wool jacket. Leather and classic style are not mutually exclusive concepts.

Wearing animal hide will always have overtones of travel, adventure, and speed, not to mention masculinity. This has much to do with the fact that clothes worn by horseback riders, coachmen, and their successors, motorcycle riders and pilots, were often made of leather. Before it became possible to waterproof textiles, leather was the only relatively water-resistant material. However, the smell of adventure which surrounds leather also impedes its entry into some circles. Blazers and tweed jackets still create a more serious impression than black leather. But neither of these is anything like as cool.

The number of potential combinations is considerable. A black, nappa blouson jacket paired with cargo pants and working boots will be just as suitable for a club tour as for Sunday breakfast in a café. A suitable alternative exists even for someone more conservative: A brown, bomber jacket with a fur-trimmed collar creates a sophisticated Ivy League look when teamed with chinos and cordovan leather boat shoes, and this combination would even be considered suitable for work in some jobs—as would the shirt jacket of rust-red velour leather, which, when worn over a shirt, necktie and knitted vest, offers an alternative to the sports jacket.

This hip-length smooth leather jacket is full of Seventies charm.

The combination of leather jacket and jeans is the favorite outfit of countless men who do not like suits or sports jackets. Even large numbers of office workers like to don this type of gear at weekends.

Hats and caps

During the past few years, hats and caps have experienced a major comeback, although this is less the case among those with more classic tastes. It seems to be mainly trendy, young people who have rediscovered a taste for hats. There is virtually no felt hat which has not—albeit briefly—enjoyed a revival in popularity, be it a fedora, a homburg, a pork pie hat, a tweed, or a derby. However, the most

The soft sports hat was a unisex classic back in the 1970s and is popular again today with young people.

Anyone who has grown out of his baseball cap might like to try a flat cap, which is more suited to older "boys" and very cool.

A Russian-style fur hat is great for keeping your ears warm and very popular with young people.

Baseball may not be a top international sport but the baseball cap is worn all around the world.

enduring fashion revival seems to have been the revival in popularity of the "trilby." The latest popular form of this classic gentleman's hat with its relatively narrow brim bears only a distant resemblance to the brown trilby which was traditionally made by London hat-makers, such as Lock & Co. or Christy's. The fashionable trilby is now available in a variety of colors, often trimmed with a contrasting hatband. It is less likely to be worn as an accessory to a suit or coat than as part of a smart, casual look. Any style of hat will keep your head warm in winter and protect it from both rain and sun. One disadvantage of a hat is that it is difficult to stow away if you are not wearing it, which is why caps are also very popular.

The brown trilby was once the trademark of a respected gentleman. Nowadays, it is given an ironic twist by young men wearing jeans and cardigans.

The Basque beret used to be favored by artists, intellectuals, and teachers but in modern times it celebrates the "nerd look."

A knitted, woolen hat looks both cool and rustic. It is also sporty, masculine, and practical— but never stuffy.

Fleecy, wool hats are warm in winter and look smarter than knitted hats. They are just as easily stuffed into a pocket.

Knitwear: the basics

1 THE MATERIAL Knitwear is basically governed by the same golden rule that you should only buy natural fibers—in other words, wool, cashmere, or cotton. Exceptions to this rule are permitted as long as the ratio of synthetics is limited. A mix with 20 percent Lycra, for example, can prevent a turtle-neck from stretching while the synthetic content remains virtually undetectable—unless you happen to be one of those fanatics whose blood runs cold at the mere thought of nylon. With such individuals, it is often more the thought of a synthetic fiber that upsets them than an actual awareness of it. Even textile experts are unable to detect small amounts of synthetics in a fabric.

TIP: Pilling can occur when short (in other words, cheap) fibers of fabric come to the surface and tangle together into little balls.

When the thread consists of long fibers, which are also twisted (by interweaving several threads), pilling does not occur. However, long fibers are more expensive, so pilling can only be avoided by having to spend more money.

2 CUT AND DIFFERENT STYLES There are many different forms and styles of knitted goods to choose from. Knitted garments, which can be combined with a shirt or polo shirt, are generally slightly more formal. The V-necked sweater, for example, is a classic item of elegant, casual clothing. Some sweaters are not worn with a shirt or, if they are, the shirt is not visible, and these are traditionally the most sporty and most casual styles of knitwear. The turtle-neck sweater is a typical example: It was originally worn to work by fishermen and sailors. Cotton is

A turtle-neck sweater keeps the neck nice and warm.

Every man's favorite— a half-zip troyer sweater.

considered the most athletic of the various materials, whereas wool and cashmere are the more elegant options.

TIP: Slim-fitting sweaters are better suited to the younger buyer. Looser styles, on the other hand, may be considered rather old-fashioned and less attractive. What a sweater looks like on the wearer depends mainly on how slim he is. If you happen to be a little overweight around the belly or hips, a wider-fitting style is best.

3 PRICE AND QUALITY Buying knitwear is a tricky business. Even the princely cashmere sweater can cause disappointment after a few weeks if it begins pilling. On the other hand, some cheap sweaters may wear extremely well for many years. Equally, cheap knitwear may, after a short time, become loose, stretch, and lose its shape. So how do you choose?

With sweaters especially, the price-quality ratio is very important. If a sweater costing 20 dollars lasts a year, then, theoretically, a 200-dollar sweater should last for ten years at the same rate of wear (i.e. worn as often each month, for example). This is clearly too much to ask of a top-quality sweater, since even the best knitwear depreciates considerably after three to five years. From a purely financial point of view, the best bet would be to buy something in the middle to lower price ranges, bearing in mind that sweaters often come to an end prematurely as a result of stains, burn holes, or moths. Expensive items are only worth the outlay if they can be given a bit of extra care. But all the care in the world cannot protect them from an overturned glass of red wine or a glowing cigarette end.

TIP: The same rules that apply to suits also apply to knitwear: Either buy relatively cheap products more frequently or else buy the absolute best. Should the expensive garment give up the ghost prematurely, a good retailer will be happy to claim compensation on your behalf from the supplier.

A sweater with a shawl collar is ideal for wearing with a scarf.

The V-neck sweater lends itself to different combinations.

A long-sleeved polo shirt of top-quality cotton is ideal for warmer days and is lighter than its piqué counterpart.

The sleeveless pullover is the closest alternative to a suit vest and can, therefore, also be combined with a double-breasted suit.

The points of the collar may be worn outside the V-neck sweater.

A thick sweater with a high collar—either with a button fastening or a turtle neck—is ideal for cool, autumn days.

V-neck pullovers are a classic basic of a gentleman's leisurewear wardrobe. Worn with a T-shirt, they reflect a modern, urban look.

Even if worn without a shirt, an elegant knitted pullover with a polo-shirt collar looks more dressed-up than the round-neck style of sweater.

Knitted jackets (or cardigans) have become hugely popular since their design adopted a more body-hugging style.

A T-shirt-style sweater is pure understatement. Made from finest cashmere, it feels as light as silk to wear.

Functional fibers

It is quite remarkable, but when men buy socks, they view even the tiniest bit of synthetic mix with extreme disapproval. There is a deep-seated fear that other people might notice they're wearing something made with synthetic fibers. This has its roots in the fact that people's initial experiences with synthetics in the 1960s and 1970s were not all that positive. Synthetic fibers made people sweat heavily, the clothes were scratchy and uncomfortable and, what was worse, the materials were not even pleasant to touch. Those who did not live through this era will have heard stories about it from their families. Synthetic fibers are associated with poorly made clothing, often in tasteless colors. Outdoor clothing and sportswear departments view synthetic fibers much more favorably, describing them as "functional" or "functional fibers," terms which have a pleasanter ring than "chemical fibers." Some of the characteristic advantages of synthetics (they are not always woven fabrics) are that they are waterproof, fast-drying, and stretchable. Modern products have very little in common with earlier types of synthetics. The level of comfort is actually greater in specialized clothing for endurance athletes or water sports enthusiasts, for example, than in fabrics made from natural fibers. Nonetheless, nature still

Antimicrobial means that fungus or bacteria are inhibited from growing, thus preventing odor. Used for socks and underwear.

Breathable means that moisture—in other words, sweat—can pass to the surface of the fabric (wicking).

Hollow fibers contain air and provide lightness and insulation.

Membrane is a very thin layer of synthetic material (e.g. Teflon coating) which provides waterproofing between the outer fabric and the lining.

Micro-encapsulation is a process for trapping tiny droplets of liquid within a fabric, e.g. fragrances.

Micro-fibers are very thin synthetic fibers (up to one hundred times finer than a human hair) which are particularly good at absorbing moisture, and are soft and light.

Neoprene is a synthetic rubber made from chloroprene, originally used in water sports.

Non-woven is an overall term for fabrics that are not woven. The fibers are bonded together by solvent, for example.

manages to produce materials which have not yet been bettered in the laboratory. One drawback with synthetic fibers is, of course, that they are still predominantly made from irreplaceable raw materials. Consequently, the amateur sportsman may feel more relaxed jogging in a cotton T-shirt and exercise pants.

Industry remains unimpressed by such objections. It is constantly developing new kinds of materials, which frequently find their way from specialized sports arenas or weatherproof clothing into everyday fashion.

Here is a summary of the most important properties, fibers, and fabrics.

Modern running gear absorbs and transports moisture away from the body, thereby shielding it from rain.

Polyacrylics are soft, fluffy, and elastic, known to us as artificial fur and fleecy fabrics.

Polyamide lends durability and strength to other fibers, e.g. Nylon, Kevlar.

Polyesters give other fibers strength, often as an additive to cotton, e.g. Trevira, Dacron, Diolen.

Polyurethane gives added elasticity to fabrics, e.g. Spandex.

Ripstop makes fabrics resistant to ripping and tearing.

Spandex (or Elastane) makes clothing stretchable and is good for sports wear. Most everyday clothing with a Spandex content is limited to women's fashion, although stretch jeans are also popular in menswear.

Stretch means elasticity and describes the elastic fibers which are mixed with the natural materials.

Techno-Naturals is a more colorful name for mixed fabrics. The name is intended to suggest that the properties of natural fibers are improved as a result of the addition of synthetics.

JUST A FEW BASICS MAKE YOU LOOK GOOD AT WORK AND IN YOUR SPARE TIME.

What we need

Just imagine what it would be like suddenly to find all your clothes gone. Many of us would shudder at the prospect of such a nightmare scenario but some people have actually had to face the terrible reality of losing everything they own as a result of war or a natural disaster. These people would of course be unimpressed by such musings. However, those of us lucky enough to live in an affluent society might do well to visualize how it would be if we no longer had a bulging wardrobe at our disposal.

In my opinion, the basic essentials of any wardrobe are the clothes we would need to replace in the event of such a loss—in other words, the clothes which experience has shown us to be indispensable. In many cases, our wardrobes often contain suits, sports jackets, pants, and shirts which never get worn and simply take up space.

The items we need to include in this list of essentials rather depend on the nature of our work. Someone responsible for training managerial executives, for example, would mostly wear a suit, but if he is often out and about, involved in customer acquisition or consultations, a more likely choice would be a blazer and pants. In a case such as this, a basic wardrobe should comprise several suits, as well as a few blazers.

As a point of principle, a distinction should be made between work clothes and leisurewear. Depending on your job, you will need three to five suits, as well as a range of leisurewear comprising three pairs of jeans, three pairs of chinos, and, possibly, two pairs of corduroy pants. If you do not have to dress for work in the traditional sense, you can probably get away with just one suit in your wardrobe, reserved for special occasions. It is a good idea, therefore, to analyze your personal lifestyle before planning a wardrobe. If it transpires that the main requirement is for suits, then choose good-quality ones wherever possible. Not only do we spend a great deal of time in and with them, but they are also a first-rate visiting card.

Shirts are the components of the basic wardrobe which usually have to be replaced most often. However, this should not be seen as an excuse to compromise on quality.

Choosing the correct business wardrobe

Tidiness, organization, and keeping order are all useful practices. Frequent sorting through your clothes and systematic purchasing will reduce your wardrobe to the essentials. This will save space and make it quicker to choose what to wear. In this way, you will eventually reach a point when it is no longer necessary to weed out any more clothes, as each garment will be serving a specific purpose.

Anyone who wears a suit to work will generally keep his business attire separate from the rest of his clothes, or at least view it as a separate category. This makes good sense since business clothes, e.g. for a job in a bank or office, are chosen according to different criteria than leisurewear.

A person's business wardrobe reveals where he comes from and where he hopes to go. Clothes can, of course, be chosen with the intention of faking a particular background. However, it is far better to stick to what is authentic. What clothes must do, however, is signal the way ahead. One's suit, shirt, necktie, and shoes must demonstrate that the wearer is worthy of a

The dark gray suit: a core piece for office and evening wear.

A blue, fine-stripe shirt: a must for Phase 2.

114 | The basic wardrobe

senior position, or at least aspires to one. It is also advisable for a person's business attire to express competence, confidence, and a cosmopolitan outlook. Colleagues and business partners might easily draw the wrong conclusions from a badly chosen necktie: If a person is incapable of selecting the appropriate tie to go with a shirt, then maybe he is not all that good at his job either.

Anyone who enjoys wearing a suit probably looked forward to wearing a good-quality, single-breasted or double-breasted suit to the office each day. Unfortunately, such early enthusiasm generally tends to dwindle in most men, which is why a well-ordered wardrobe removes the need to spend a long time thinking about which suit to wear. This may well lead to a resurgence of pleasure in wearing a smart outfit.

1 st phase: Establish the basics and only focus on the essentials. Tried-and-true outfits are best. No experiments. This also means avoiding the temptation to make impulsive purchases in the sales. Always stick to the plan.

2 nd phase: Augment and complete. Once the fundamentals are in place, any gaps can be filled. In this way, you can create your own personal style.

3 rd phase: Make occasional additions. You can now cut back on your budget. The main investment has been made and the important thing now is to conserve, maintain, and complete. Major purchases will become more infrequent and it will be mostly smaller items which need replacing.

A suit and vest also look good on the younger man.

Business casual: the sports jacket (all photos: Scabal).

The basic

You do not need to start your working life with lots of different clothes. The emphasis should be first and foremost on quality, particularly if the budget is limited. Two suits, a few shirts and neckties, two pairs of black lace-ups (preferably welt-stitched), and two coats would be enough to begin with. If these garments are carefully looked after, they will last a good while.

business essentials

A dark gray suit with a white shirt and muted necktie is the perfect choice for daytime business appointments or for a formal evening event and should be worn with black shoes. Double buckles are an eye-catching option.

A medium-gray suit in a soft material is ideal for the office. Teaming it with a light-blue shirt, dark-blue silk necktie, and brown suede leather shoes creates a classic Italian look. Worn with black shoes, it would also be suitable for evening wear.

London bankers are still fond of wearing a chalk-stripe, navy-blue suit—often double-breasted. This is combined with a polka-dot navy necktie (unless a regimental or club tie is appropriate). A classic pair of Oxfords would typically complete this outfit.

The US-style business look: a two-button, single-breasted, navy-blue suit made from lightweight, high-twist wool, worn with a classic, striped shirt and a necktie in a distinctive color, e.g. red. These could be combined with a pair of hand-stitched penny loafers—"Made in the USA," naturally—as a concession to American casual style.

An autumn variation of the blazer-chinos combination comprises an unlined blazer of fairly heavy wool, pants of robust twill, a plaid shirt and a thick, coarse, wool tie. If the occasion permits, brown slip-on shoes may be worn. Although not suitable for business wear, they nevertheless look best with this outfit.

A single- or double-breasted blazer is an essential wardrobe item for less formal business occasions. A blue jacket combined with cotton pants, a discreetly patterned shirt, a muted tie and penny loafers would be typical examples of a business-casual outfit.

Business-casual in summer for less formal meetings or everyday office wear without important meetings: a light-colored, plaid sports jacket of fine worsted cloth, light-colored cotton pants, striped shirt, wine-red necktie of knitted silk—as a contrast to the sporty look of the other elements—and classic, Oxford-style lace-ups.

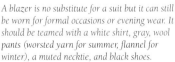

A blazer is no substitute for a suit but it can still be worn for formal occasions or evening wear. It should be teamed with a white shirt, gray, wool pants (worsted yarn for summer, flannel for winter), a muted necktie, and black shoes.

Tweed jacket: an indispensable basic which is more important than the suit.

Blazer or sports jacket: a preppy classic.

Gray wool: indispensable for a smart look.

Corduroy pants: the king of casual pants.

Moleskin pants: the winter equivalent of chinos.

Black penny loafers: casual Sunday and office shoes.

The penny loafer: slip-on shoe with youthful charm.

essentials

If in doubt, a shirt is smarter than any other type of leisure shirt.

A lightweight, quilted jacket is ideal when the weather turns cool.

Smart and functional: the waterproof field coat.

Brown chukka boots are robust and classy.

Suede lace-up shoes: the all-rounder for stylish leisurewear.

Coats

(left) The green loden coat is as popular in Milan and Paris as it is in Austria, where it originated. (above) The covert coat is a favorite of Anglophiles.

(right) Because of its longer length, this field coat is classed as a coat rather than a jacket. It is more waterproof than its waxed cotton counterpart and is much warmer. Furthermore, the tweed fabric gives it a more elegant appearance.

(below) This single-breasted, slip-on coat in cotton gabardine with raglan sleeves is the civilian alternative to the trench coat.

Casual

Bermuda shorts: leisurewear for hot summer days.

The T-shirt should only be worn in very informal company.

The polo shirt is a more stylish version of the T-shirt.

Jeans: Brand names like Levis, Lee, or Wrangler are the most authentic.

An excellent modification: a polo shirt with long sleeves.

The standard British leisurewear garment.

Chinos: lighter than jeans and more appropriate in many situations.

Boat shoes with a raised sole: yuppies all over the world unite!

Driving shoes with studded sole: slightly more sophisticated than the boat shoe.

The leather jacket: a favorite with some more macho types of men.

Top-quality sneakers as a more elegant alternative to Converse All Stars.

A short, cotton windbreaker gives good protection when the weather turns cool.

A lightweight anorak style is the perfect option on cool, wet days.

Boat shoes are a must, even if you are not a sailor.

The basic wardrobe | 127

It's all about looking good

The colors we wear can have a decisive influence on our
outward appearance. A pale blond man wearing a beige
summer suit and white shirt, for example, can end up
looking very unprepossessing. It is common knowledge
that the way colors and patterns are coordinated is also
key to the right image. What is less widely known is that
proportions are also one of the prime factors which determine what sort of impression we make in our clothes.
Squat, stout, slender, young, old, confident, or clown-
ish—our appearance depends largely on whether our
clothes emphasize our good points and conceal our prob-
lem areas. An "off-the-peg" suit may be well-proportioned
in itself but may not flatter the wearer's figure once he has it on.

Good custom tailors are past masters at dealing with proportions. Clothes designers also have a good grasp of the subject and will certainly try to optimize a garment's
proportions—although this only applies to ready-to-wear sizes and not to the idiosyn-
crasies of individual figures. A custom tailor must adapt what are essentially the same
basic suit models to different body shapes in a way that will flatter whatever figure he
is presented with. A double-breasted suit in Size 38 should fit all men of a medium
build with a chest measurement of 38 inches (96 cm), whether or not they have long
or short arms, a broad pelvis or narrow hips, a hollow back or hunched shoulders. A
custom tailor can optimize the fit of a double-breasted suit to take account of any of
these eventualities.

Just because someone has a good grasp of proportions, however, does not mean they
can perform miracles. Not even the best custom tailor can turn a short, fat person into
someone who is tall and slender, but a master of the art of proportions will be able to
give a barrel-shaped client at least the fleeting illusion of a waist, broad chest, and slim
legs. Anyone who knows the basic rules relating to the question of proportions will be
able to avoid many mistakes when buying "off the peg."

*Everyone perceives red and green differently, which makes colors almost as difficult to discuss as
emotions. That is why color samples are so essential.*

The human body and the golden ratio

The golden ratio is based on what classical scholars regarded as the ideal proportions for measurements in architecture and art. Greek temples were built according to this principle and are, to this day, regarded as examples of perfect architectural proportion. Two lines are said to be in a golden ratio when the longer line divided by the shorter line is also equal to the whole length divided by the longer line.

A simplified version of this ratio can also be applied to the human body. The different parts of each human body can be divided into ideal proportional sections (vertical and horizontal). Generally, this results in each human body being harmoniously proportioned. The individual lines provide the key to how clothes fit.

To find the dividing lines, the body is divided horizontally into eight equal sections. The head constitutes ⅛th of the body's length. The most harmonious and, in golden ratio terms, aesthetically pleasing central point is located at ⅝ of the body's length.

Take this concrete example: A body length of 5 feet 10 inches (178 cm) divided by 8 is 8¾ inches (22.25 cm). The harmonious proportions in a golden ratio would be ⅝ to ⅜ (⅝ = 3 feet 7¾ inches (111.25 cm), ⅜ = 2 feet 2¼ inches (66.75 cm)). The ideal central point would be at ⅝ of the body length = 3 feet 7¾ inches (111.25 cm).

As a rule, the dividing lines can be pinpointed to parts of the body, e.g. nipples, coccyx, middle of the knee, etc. With classic sports or suit jackets and blazers, the button fastening should be at the optical center of the body. The optimum lengths for garments are calculated from the horizontal line segments. Many tailors and designers draw on this theory in their work.

Button fastening
At navel level.

Sleeve length
Shirt cuff must project.

Jacket length
Rear must be covered.

Pants length
The pants hem should form a single crease. The narrower the pants leg, the shorter the pants.

1

2

3

4

5

6

7

8

Different types of figure

Ready-to-wear clothes will fit well if a person's measurements correspond to those of the garment in question. Unfortunately, this is rarely the case. Deviations from the norm are far more common, resulting in the typical problems that relate to a garment's fit. However, there is no need to rush straight to the made-to-measure store or custom tailor—a few optical tricks can often sort the problem out.

ACCENTUATING AND DIVIDING LINES

Horizontal lines make you look fatter and shorter, whereas vertical lines tend to elongate, therefore pinstripes are ideal for portly

Large stomach: The jacket needs more length at the front.

Upright posture: The jacket needs to be longer at the front and shorter at the back.

gentlemen. An unbroken expanse suggests volume, which thereby suggests weight. A large belly, for example, will appear smaller if the front of the shirt is broken up by a necktie.

SMALL MEN

Clothes may be slightly tight and a little short, which emphasizes the vertical lines. Pants legs should be clearly divided. Jacket button should be higher. High crotch seam and accentuated shoulders and waist.

TALL MEN

Clothes may be a little looser and horizontal lines can be accentuated. Break up large, unbroken areas.

AND FINALLY

Bear in mind the head-to-shoulders ratio and adapt the cut of the pants to the shape of the belly. By skillfully balancing the "weight" of light and dark colors you can optically alter the length of short legs or a long torso.

Stooped posture: needs more length at the back so that the jacket does not look too short.

Athletic figure: problematical, as the upper body looks out of proportion to the hip width.

Combining colors and patterns

Whenever I address audiences in my native Germany, the questions nearly always revolve around what is allowed and not allowed—including in matters of color and pattern. German people love rules—a cliché, maybe, but true nevertheless. Men, in particular, want clear answers to what are, for them, difficult questions, such as whether a bottle-green necktie goes with a dark-blue suit. Some also want to know whether a particular color can be teamed with this or that shade. What is needed here are some clear guidelines. Every country is different. For example, a talk I once gave in the Netherlands on the most important rules governing men's style was greeted with no more than polite applause. The same talk in Germany was met instead with real enthusiasm and followed by a lively question session. Alternative subjects also have to be devised for British and Italian audiences, who would consider a talk on rules simply too boring. Nonetheless, rules can help less fashion-conscious men, especially, to find their way around in a confusing world.

COLOR WHEEL AND COLOR COMBINATION

Most of us can possibly still remember the color wheel from art lessons at school. Only a few people realize that it can be a useful aid in combining colors. Especially, if this is something we are unsure about.

If we look at the color wheel, we can see two things: firstly, that there is an almost

continuous flow of color between the three primary colors of red, yellow, and blue if the adjoining shades are mixed together. Secondly, complementary pairs of colors can occur in an almost infinite number of variations, all of which look good and can help us to combine colors.

HARMONIOUS COLOR COMBINATIONS

Not very daring but always a safe choice are combinations of colors which occur next to each other on the color wheel. In other words, adjoining blue tones can always be paired with a dark-blue suit. In practical terms, this means that we can always team a dark-blue suit with a light-blue shirt and violet necktie. A brown corduroy sports jacket would similarly look very good with beige pants.

COMPLEMENTARY COMBINATIONS

If you look at the colors on the opposite page, you will no doubt recognize all kinds of color combinations from your own wardrobe, be it stripes on neckties, shirts, scarves, or even the pattern on a sweater. Perfectly harmonious color pairings are in evidence everywhere. It suddenly becomes clear why some designers are so keen to put orange and blue, or green and red together in their necktie designs.

WHAT ABOUT BROWN AND GRAY?

Although very common in the fashion industry, the color wheel does not contain brown or gray. A closer look at the colors they contain will help you decide what to combine them with. Brown, for instance, contains traces of red, orange, or violet while gray often has blue or lilac overtones. These form a starting point for combinations with other colors. As a rule of thumb, brown and gray go very well with navy and bottle green.

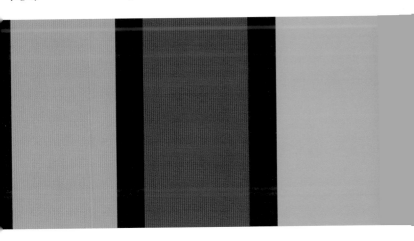

The most important color groups

THE COUNTRY LOOK

Earth and plant colors, such as brown, rust, and all shades of green, i.e. moss, pine, and grass colors, dominate this group. Plant colors also include wheat yellow, lilac, poppy red, and sunflower yellow. A common mistake is to ignore "real" colors and only use browns and greens, which risk making you look like a hunter. Although there is nothing necessarily wrong with that, a hunter's outfit is designed for quite a specific purpose. A city-dweller visiting the country does not need to look as if he is going hunting. Gray and black are unacceptable colors for country wear, while dark blue should be worn sparingly and only in combination with other colors, e.g. a

navy-blue blazer with mustard-yellow pants and nut-brown shoes.

THE BUSINESS LOOK

Gray, black, or dark blue are the correct colors for business wear. However, only the suit should be gray, never the shirt. Dark blue is suitable for both suit and necktie, whereas only lighter blues are permissible for the shirt. The only black items in your business wardrobe should be shoes and knee-length socks—black is inappropriate for suits or shirts. Despite their popularity with designers, black suits have no place in your business wardrobe (unless you happen to be a funeral director). Brown is not acceptable in any form—not even in Italy, although many people believe that combining brown shoes with a dark suit creates a typically Italian look. Necktie

colors can be somewhat bolder. But, the more senior your position within the firm, the more muted your necktie should be.

THE PREPPY LOOK

The preppy look has quite recently begun to develop a rather trendy reputation. This style, which is now a familiar concept to most people, reflects the kind of college fashion which American men's outfitters, such as Brooks Brothers, have been offering, virtually unchanged, since the 1930s. Typical preppy style includes bold, strong colors which are teamed with more muted shades of khaki, stone, sand, or white. Also typical are all shades of blue, from light-blue Oxford shirts with seersucker suits to dark, navy-blue blazers. Any shade of brown is also acceptable. The preppy look permits bold color combinations, such as yellow and green, red and blue, or orange and light blue.

EVENING

In the early 19th century, the legendary English dandy, Beau Brummel, adopted black as the obligatory color for men's evening wear so as to show off the ladies' dresses better. Ever since then, gentlemen's evening wear has been based on this stark black-and-white contrast. This applies equally both to the tuxedo and to tails. Any attempts to introduce colored bow ties or shirts have ended in failure. The only way to add color is in small amounts, e.g. in the form of a lining, socks, or a pocket handkerchief. One option for tuxedo fans, perhaps, is a black suit combined with a white shirt. This could be worn either with an open collar or a black necktie. Purists will lament the absence of midnight blue, a shade which is supposed to look even blacker than black, and often cited as the true color for a tuxedo. However, the fact remains: Black is the only color for nighttime elegance.

Belvest, the Italian suit manufacturer, includes a wide range of styles in its collection.

The right necktie

Many men have great difficulty coordinating a necktie with the rest of their clothes, i.e. the suit and shirt. Needless to say, there are some fundamental and practical rules on mixing colors and patterns. Once you have grasped these, you will never again find yourself standing helplessly in front of the wardrobe with a necktie in your hand. You will be able to reach confidently and purposefully for the right suit and shirt.

1 *Start with the biggest item first.* The larger the garment, the more it will have cost and the fewer items like it you will have in your wardrobe, so decide first which suit you are going to wear. Let us assume it is dark gray. Lay it on the bed.

The shirt is the next biggest element. What will go with a dark gray suit? Light blue, white, pink, blue stripes, or checks on white. You opt for light blue. Place it on top of the suit.

Now for the necktie (or bow tie). What goes with dark gray (suit) and light blue (shirt)? Almost everything: dark blue, wine red, pink, yellow, lime green, any kind of stripe, or even a little pattern. Choose whichever color you fancy and then lay the necktie with the suit and shirt. The result: a perfectly coordinated combination of suit, shirt, and necktie.

2 *Patterned with unpatterned, and tiny patterns with large patterns.* It all looks so perfect in the store window of the men's outfitters: checked suit, striped shirt, diamond-pattern necktie. But what happens if you buy one of these items and find, when you get home, that nothing else in your wardrobe goes with it? There are only two basic principles to remember in this respect:

PATTERNED WITH UNPATTERNED

Here is an example, by way of clarification: You have selected a blue, pinstripe suit—in other words, something patterned, which can invariably be teamed with something unpatterned. Suppose we select a light-blue shirt. Since the suit is the main part of the outfit, the necktie should likewise be a uniform color—in other words, unpatterned, for instance in pink. You may have seen this combination a dozen times before but now you know the principles behind it and, above all, why it looks so good.

SMALL PATTERNS WITH LARGE PATTERNS

If we take a closer look at the stripes on a suit, we will see that the distance between them is generally just under half an inch (1 cm). In other words, the pattern is relatively small, which means, therefore, that we can combine it with a shirt with a large pattern—either of stripes, at least an inch apart, or better still, a large check, e.g. dark blue on white or pale blue. According to Rule 1 (patterned with unpatterned), it should be teamed with a plain necktie, which will not clash either with the suit or the shirt. And the color? Entirely a matter of individual taste. A blue suit and blue-and-white check shirt would be perfectly complemented by a vivid pink necktie or even a bright-yellow one.

3 *Harmony and contrast.* Gray mouse or parrot? The ideal color combination lies somewhere in between these two extremes. The important factor here is getting the right mix. Contrasting colors will add a spark to harmony while, conversely, balanced colors will soften strong contrasts.

Here is another example: dark-blue suit, light-blue shirt—a harmonious combination. A dark-blue necktie would blend perfectly with this outfit but the final effect would be rather dull. Fresh orange would create exactly the right amount of contrast. Teaming a dark-blue suit with a white shirt already creates a striking contrast, so adding a bright-red necktie to the ensemble could well make the whole thing resemble a carnival costume. A necktie in powder pink, light blue, or grass green would be much easier on the eye. Which would be the most suitable color depends on individual skin tone. Light blue would be best for pale-skinned types, while pink-cheeked individuals would be better off with green. Only darker-skinned men could choose any of these colors.

Color and type

Colors do, without doubt, exert some kind of influence although experts are still not sure how. Nor is it clear who these experts actually are—do we mean psychologists, doctors, hairdressers, artists, designers, behavioral researchers, fashion retailers, or counselors? And what about physicists? Do they not know more about the subject than anyone else?

It is fairly safe to assume that research has indeed produced some incontrovertible evidence on the effect of colors. However, some of what these color experts postulate does not always stand up to close inspection. Nor is it even necessary to delve too deep. Over the centuries, artists, architects, tailors, and fashion designers have amassed enough concrete experience to provide some reliable indicators. What has, in fact, emerged is that people can be divided, according to their skin and hair color, into groups: for example, the blond, Scandinavian type, the dark-haired, dark-eyed southern European, or the dark-skinned African. Most methods of color counseling are based on these different

Dark hair, dark skin:
American jazz musician, Wynton Marsalis.

Light-colored hair and skin:
Prince Bernhard of Baden.

groups. Women, in particular, frequently have a problem in this respect: many of those who wish to be analyzed in terms of their skin or hair color are not actually revealing their natural color. Cosmetics, tanning studios, or fake tans are responsible for altering one's true complexion, while hair may be artificially colored, toned, lightened, curled, or straightened. A pale-skinned, blue-eyed, blond, northern European woman may suddenly acquire the complexion and hair color of an Italian. If her clothes are then color-matched to this artificially created type, the result can sometimes be quite strange.

These days, it is acceptable for men to pluck their eyebrows, remove body hair, go to the solarium, and use toner on their hair. Compared to most women, however, they are far less adventurous and the majority would never dream of altering their hair or skin color. Consequently, men are better subjects to study with regard to color. The results will inevitably be more authentic if the person being styled is someone with natural red hair, pale skin, freckles, and brown eyes rather than someone who colors his hair black, then tries to coordinate his clothes with this artificial veneer. Natural hair color is always the best match for your skin, which is why women with black hair that has been bleached look just as unnatural as blondes who have colored their hair black.

Pink complexion and hair with a reddish tinge: businessman and designer, Lapo Elkann.

Dark hair and skin that tans easily: Felipe of Spain.

When I give talks or lectures, I often get asked by male members of the audience which colors suit them and which do not. They are conscious that they feel comfortable and look good in some outfits but not in others. If I were a color consultant, I would offer these gentlemen a comprehensive consultation. They would receive an analysis of their specific type, together with appropriate recommendations with regard to specific colors. However, since I am not a color consultant but someone who is interested in various aspects of clothes and their impact, I will pass on two, simple, easy-to-follow tips:

CONTRAST

Look in the mirror. Is the contrast between your skin and your hair color pronounced or insignificant? Pale skin and black hair produce maximum contrast, while the contrast between dark skin and dark hair is only minimal (the same is true for pale-skinned types with white-blond hair).

The degree of contrast between skin and hair should be echoed in your clothes. In the case of business wear, a white shirt and dark suit are best suited to light-colored skin and black hair. The necktie should also stand out clearly from the shirt. Less of a contrast between your face and hair also means that less of a contrast is required in your clothing, so you could, for example, wear a light-blue shirt with a medium-gray suit. Why? Your face and hair should be all of a piece with your clothes. If strongly contrasting clothes are worn by someone without much contrast between skin and

This tweed coat by Henry Poole & Co. of London would suit the coloring of a fair-haired, rosy-cheeked man—i.e. whose skin and hair do not pose too much of a contrast.

hair color, the face will recede into the background and appear even paler. Conversely, striking contrasts around the face will be subdued and diluted by muted contrasts on the clothing front.

COLORS

Some skin tones and hair coloring are very striking, while others are less distinctive. Color, where it exists, should be accentuated—either by echoing the same color in your clothing, especially around the face, or by introducing complementary contrasts. The blue of someone's eyes, for example, can be picked out in a necktie, red hair in the checks on a jacket. An alternative to mirroring facial tones would be to inject complementary contrasts. These contrasts occur between colors which lie opposite each other on the color wheel. For example, typical pairings include violet and yellow, blue and orange, or green and red.

A complementary contrast also signifies that the two colors in the pairing harmonize perfectly and help augment the impact of the other. However, a decision usually involves more than just simple, basic colors, which is why it can help to view a more elaborate color wheel, subdivided into lots more shades and showing a wider range of complementary color contrasts.

Various different greens would go well with red hair, for example, and choosing precisely the right shade would require careful consideration. Rust-red hair, for instance, would be greatly enhanced by olive green.

The mix of black and white in this Glen plaid would be perfect for a southern European type who is turning gray, as it would tone with the muted contrasts of his coloring.

BOTH RULING PASSION AND OBJECT OF DESIRE—SHOES
ARE THE KEY TO ACHIEVING THE RIGHT LOOK.

Shoes

Shoes are quite simply the basis of a perfect appearance. In formal or business wear,
welt-stitched shoes are considered the call-
ing card of a stylishly dressed gentleman.
But regardless of the particular style of
dress, footwear is an important part of the
overall image. A rocker wearing sandals
will simply not be a rocker. And young
fashion would be lost without the right
kind of sneakers.

Sneakers (or "trainers" in British English) were originally sports shoes, but are
now a type of footwear which has about
as much to do with sports as a Porsche Cayenne has to do with mud and impassable
terrain. The only thing sneakers have in common with a sports shoe is their shape and
the predominantly synthetic material from which they are made—and, of course, how
they fit. This type of shoe either cocoons the foot in cotton wool or else provides no
shock absorption at all. Sneakers do not keep the feet warm in the way that leather
shoes do—in summer, they are much too hot and make your feet sweat, and in winter, your feet get frozen stiff. Yet many men persist in wearing sneakers most of the
time—and not just during their school or student days.

Such people often take their first steps toward the "correct" kind of shoe when they
switch to boots. Classic US brands of sturdy working shoes, in particular, tend to con-
vert sneaker enthusiasts to a preference for shoes which offer support and protection
and which are also good at regulating foot temperature. Some of them will eventually
aspire to the king of shoes, the welt-stitched model. If these are a good fit, they will
feel as light and comfortable as any sports shoe and will also be better for the foot and
considerably longer-lasting.

*Your shoe wardrobe should have a style to fit every occasion: a moccasin, for example by Gucci (left),
for summer leisurewear and a pair of sturdy lace-ups to accompany a sports jacket or suit.*

The main styles

Name: Derby. Colors/upper material: brown or black calfskin, or cordovan. Suede only in shades of brown. History/origins: Open lacing lends the Derby a more sporting appearance, hence its name. Its design originates from the open-laced boots worn by soldiers serving under the Prussian field marshal Blücher, which is why they are also known as Bluchers. Style: a slightly casual lace-up. When to wear: depending on color and outfit, suitable for business and formal occasions (in black with a thin leather sole) or for leisurewear (in brown). Special features: The laces should be threaded in the criss-cross method.

Name: Brogue. The term "Budapests" sometimes used is misleading as this type of shoe did not originate in Budapest. It is, however, traditionally popular with Hungarian shoemakers. Colors/upper material: black or brown calfskin, more often cordovan in the USA. Brown suede is also typical. History/origins: The brogue has its rural origins in Scotland. It established itself as a casual shoe in the early 20th century. Style: a sturdy British shoe. When to wear: in brown: as part of an English country look. In black: suitable for business. Special features: Its decorative perforations make the black brogue unsuitable for formal occasions.

Name: the Oxford (or Balmoral). Colors/upper material: black or brown calfskin, occasionally horsehide (cordovan). Suede models only in brown. History/origins: The Oxford was developed in England in the late 19th century from a half-boot which gave it its name but did not itself survive. Style: the most formal men's shoe to wear with a suit. When to wear: business, or special occasions. Special features: black Oxfords (with or without a toecap) can also be worn with a morning coat. The Oxford's thin leather sole makes it the most elegant men's shoe.

Name: Monk strap. Colors/upper material: cf. Oxford and Derby. History/origins: so-called because the buckles are said to recall those on monks' sandals. This shoe has been popular in its present form since the early 20th century. Style: classic, but too casual for evening wear. When to wear: business (in black) or smart casual. Special features: Perfectionists match the color of their shoe buckle to that of their belt (in other words, a brass buckle to match a gold-colored belt buckle).

Name: Loafer. Color/upper material: cf. Oxford and Derby. History/origins: Until the 1920s, slip-on shoes were only worn indoors. However, after they first appeared in the USA, loafers soon became popular as casual day shoes. Style: sporty to casually elegant. When to wear: for business and leisure. Special features: In conservative circles, the smooth, black loafer would be considered too casual to be worn for business or with a dark suit.

Name: Chukka boot. Colors/upper material: brown calfskin (usually suede), or cordovan, very occasionally smooth, black leather. History/origins: casual ankle boot worn by English polo players. Style: a shoe like a Range Rover, the perfect accompaniment to tweed, corduroy, and a waxed jacket. When to wear: for a country look or leisure activities. Special features: Trendy Italians also wear them for business with a gray flannel suit.

Name: Boat shoe. Colors/upper material: brown, dark blue, white or in white-brown or white-blue combinations. History/origins: developed for sailors (slip-proof sole). The construction of the shoe upper is based on the Indian moccasin. Style: sports shoe. When to wear: for leisure activities. Special features: These shoes should be worn in summer without socks whereas in autumn, heavier styles are worn with colored or patterned socks.

Name: Sneaker. Colors/upper material: leather/textile/synthetics. History/origins: Its predecessor was the true athlete's shoe but the modern sneaker is only suitable for general wear. Style: trendily casual. When to wear: fashionable, youthful day wear, leisurewear. Special features: Sneakers are absolutely taboo with a business suit.

Name: Patent leather lace-up. Colors/upper material: black patent leather. History/origins: This is the evening version of the most formal men's shoe. Worn in the early 20th century to go with the newly invented tuxedo and dark pants. Style: very formal. When to wear: evening dress. Special features: Normal laces can be replaced with satin bows.

Name: pumps, court or opera shoes. Colors/upper material: black calfskin or patent leather with corded silk (grosgrain) bow. History/origins: the oldest men's shoe (predecessor of the women's pump) dates back to the 16th century. Style: elegant. When to wear: the only proper shoe to wear with tails or evening dress, particularly for ballroom dancing; also suitable for wear with a tuxedo. Special features: It is considered especially elegant to opt for pumps of fine calfskin and polish them to a high gloss.

Name: Velvet slipper. Colors/upper material: various colors of velvet, e.g. red, bottle green, black, violet, or blue with embroidered initials or motifs (e.g. animal heads, coats-of-arms). History/origins: cf. pumps. Constructing this from fabric, e.g. velvet or silk, is just a variation of the same style. Style: eccentric. When to wear: worn with a velvet smoking jacket (of the same color), occasionally with a black tuxedo (smoking). Wear with jeans for added eccentricity.

The loafer

People's views on the slip-on shoes known as "loafers" differ from country to country. In the US and Great Britain, the elegant, welt-stitched loafer has attracted a loyal following and is part of the classic business look. In continental Europe, however, the loafer is still regarded as not a serious contender among welt-stitched shoes. In Germany, especially, the few men who insist on top-quality shoes prefer lace-ups. Not only does this reflect a desire for solidity and reliability but also an attitude to money: "If I'm buying such expensive shoes, I want the most for my money."

This uncertainty over loafers among Germans is best illustrated by their attitude to the tassel loafer. Regarded in America as a symbol of ultra-conservative,

Black, welt-stitched penny loafers in black are acceptable with a suit but are better matched with a smart casual look.

The original loafer, inspired by the moccasin, is the well-dressed gentleman's sneaker.

The tassel loafer is fine for business wear in America, its country of origin.

(Photo center) The full-strap loafer is the most elegant version.

The pimple-sole driver's shoe is Italy's classic leisure shoe.

East-coast elegance and also worn by members of the British royal family for Sunday morning church attendance, instead this shoe is viewed in Germany as a foolish error in taste, a perception which has undoubtedly been a contributory factor in it acquiring the nickname "pom-pom shoe." German aversion to the loafer in general and the tassel loafer in particular has led to lace-ups frequently being worn with casual wear. The combination of jeans or chinos with brown brogues, which is extremely common in Germany, is rarely seen in Great Britain, the USA, or in Mediterranean countries where the loafer is generally the preferred weekend shoe. Lace-ups tend to be reserved for more formal attire.

The casual shoe

BOOTS FOR LEISUREWEAR: CASUAL, MASCULINE, AND COMFORTABLE.

Italian men are famous for being particularly well dressed. This has a good deal to do with the fact that they pay great attention to style in all aspects of life—including and especially when they are away from the office. While people in other countries prefer practical, reasonably priced, and comfortable clothes when they are not at work, Italians invest a good deal of money in casual clothing—and this includes the appropriate shoes.

Stylish, casual shoes are in the main produced in America, where the concept of leisure clothing originated in the first place. Even the British, who invented virtually every aspect of men's fashion, have been inspired by the American smart casual look. The ultimate classic shoe is the casual penny loafer, followed closely by the boat shoe. Anyone owning both of these styles is equipped for just about any leisure occasion.

The American wardrobe also provides an appropriate outfit for winter. Sturdy working and hunting boots are the first choice as much for fans of classic fashion as for fashion disciples. If cared for properly, these boots will last as long as welt-stitched shoes for the office.

Business shoes

Two or three pairs of shoes are the minimum requirement for office wear, as they should always be alternated. There is divided opinion regarding color. The English still adhere to the "no brown in town" and "no brown after six" rules, whereas the Italians and French have been ignoring these rules and wearing brown shoes with dark suits since the 1980s. There are hundreds of different shades between light sand and deep rust red. What is more, leather can also be "dark polished," as shoe experts call it—in other words, polishing a light-brown shoe with a wine-red shoe cream. However, if you want to play it safe, choose black for business wear. Bankers, in particular, would find themselves completely out of line if they turned up to meetings in London and New York wearing brown Oxfords.

The plaintip Oxford: the most formal lace-up, perfect with a dark suit.

The Oxford: the ultimate classic, formal shoe.

The Monk strap: its buckles are not to everyone's taste.

There are far more than just two style options, ranging from the Oxford, Wingtip Brogue, Derby, Monk(strap) to the Loafer—the huge number of English shoe terms is daunting for any shoe novice. However, shoes can actually be classified quite simply. Shoes with perforated hole patterns are called brogues, styles without perforations are called Oxfords or Derbys. Oxfords are shoes with a toe-cap, while the Derby is a shoe with open lacing. Monks are shoes with buckles and what some call "moccasins" are termed loafers by the shoe expert. Anyone who does not want to memorize all this, can simply point to the shoe style of his choice.

SHOE CODE RULES IN BRIEF

1. As a rule of thumb, wear black for business and evening events ("no brown after six").
2. The black Oxford is the most formal men's shoe.
3. Loafers are generally more casual.
4. The tassel loafer was originally a business shoe.
5. Always wear black shoes for funerals.
6. Patent shoes only for evening wear.

The Derby: casual but comfortable for high insteps.

The Brogue: decorative perforations make the shoe a little less formal.

The Half-brogue is better matched with heavier fabrics than Oxfords.

Cowboy boots

Hardly any other type of footwear arouses such mixed emotions as the cowboy boot. It is synonymous with freedom, adventure, masculinity, and the American dream, yet it also stands for backwoods provinciality and lack of taste. It would seem exceedingly odd for a European government leader to hold a press conference from his weekend retreat wearing a pair of riding boots. Yet, it seems entirely normal for the US President on vacation to appear before journalists wearing cowboy boots.

Cowboy boots are classic boots with a long history. They were invented at the end of the 19th century in the workshop of an unknown shoemaker somewhere in Texas or Kansas. Like blue jeans, the design of these boots was based on expediency. The high legs protect the rider from thorns, bushes, and barbed wire as well as from painful contact with the stirrups. The calf width was also made more generous than in the case of European-style riding boots so that the cowboy could, if necessary, pull off his boots quickly. The heel was designed to suit the American riding style of wedging the foot in the stirrups and provided a firm foothold on the ground for lassoing calves. The embroidery on the outside of the boot leg was originally designed to

A selection from the range of US boot manufacturer Tony Lama.

strengthen the leather but later became a decorative element.

Many of the cowboy boots sold today are produced in Spain. However, fans of the genuine article can get all they need from US manufacturers. An abundance of suppliers stock cowboy boots in a variety of price brackets, ranging from low-priced versions (with a glued-on, artificial-leather sole) to the extremely exclusive, custom-made models. There is also a market for antique cowboy boots, which can be found in specialist stores and on the Internet. A visit to a store to buy a pair of boots is well worthwhile, if only for the experience of trying on the full range.

Materials for cowboy boots

FUNCTIONAL AND DECORATIVE TYPES OF LEATHER.

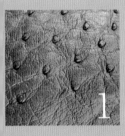

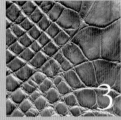

A cowboy boot, designed to be worn as footwear for work, should be made from sturdy cowhide. Hard-wearing, decorative boots can be made from embossed cowhide, e.g. with an alligator grain.

Ostrich leather (1) is very popular with amateur cowboys as it is light and breathable. Whichever part of the ostrich skin is used determines the number of characteristic pimples. Hide from ostrich legs may also be used. Snakeskin (2) is another material typically used for authentic cowboy boots. The most common snakes used for this purpose are pythons and rattlesnakes.

Snakeskin is particularly light, its pattern and structure depending on how the skin is cut—most importantly, whether it is from the back or the belly. Other commonly used skins include lizard, alligator, eel, buffalo, crocodile (3), and goat. Aardvaark skins are particularly expensive. It may seem strange to some people that such cute-looking animals are killed for their hide in order to make boots, but real cowboys are free of any such sentimentality.

Shoes: how they are made

A shoe is said to be welt-stitched when the upper leather and the inner sole are held together by a single, invisible seam. The welt—a narrow strip of leather visible on the outside of the shoe—is then stitched to the upper and inner sole. The outer sole is then attached to the welt with a visible seam. Despite what many sales staff may say, the outer sole is not in fact simply held in place by the seam but also by adhesive. This avoids any risk of the sole falling off when the sole seam is abraded.

Welt-stitched shoes are considered a symbol of elegant living and good taste. They are very expensive and beyond the means of many people, are long-lasting and good for the feet, they need a lot of care and attention, and can become a ruling passion or even a fetish. In the

The sole seam is usually visible in a welt-stitched shoe.

Glued in place: The sole is fixed to the shoe with adhesive. This is not considered a particularly high-quality method but is well suited to lightweight shoes with a thin sole.

Stitched together (also known as Blake or McKay seam): The sole is joined to the inner sole by a seam—as seen from visible stitches on the inside.

final analysis, however, welt-stitched shoes are still just shoes. Special rules apply in the case of welt-stitched shoes but their fans are still prepared to accept them. Breaking in this type of shoe may be a painful business, sometimes lasting for weeks; their leather soles absorb water and offer no protection against stony ground; their purchase will involve expensive accessories, for example shoe stretchers; and professional repairs and alterations are far more expensive than for other types of shoes. In short, welt-stitched shoes are rather like expensive sports cars, which are driven in a way that would be unforgivable in a more modest car.

Welt-stitched shoes are very rarely actually sewn by hand in the true sense of the word, so it is not really technically correct for producers of such shoes to call themselves "manufacturers." The term "factory-produced" would be more accurate. Although the shoes are constantly being handled during the various production stages, they are sewn entirely by machine. Only shoemakers producing custom-made shoes actually sew by hand using a needle and thread. Decorative seams may occasionally be added by hand in the factory.

Viewed from above without its outer sole, the welt is clearly visible. This will later be abraded (photo supplied by Schuh Konzept, Berlin).

This view of a welt-stitched shoe without its outer sole shows the cork filler and the wooden central support (photo supplied by Schuh Konzept, Berlin).

Superga or
Chic or

Mens' fashion in the 21st century is a succession of major or minor trends. Specifically, the changes involve the cut and silhouette: Sometimes styles are very loose, sometimes very close-fitting. In the broader sense, the changes often reflect past eras and encompass fashion revivals and new discoveries. The different fashion eras—a designer's treasure trove of revival possibilities—are closely associated with the countries which set the styles during these periods.

America dominated the 1950s, when it was all about denim, rock 'n' roll, leather jackets, youth fashion, and, in a cultural sense, the Beatnik look. In the 1960s, it was Great Britain which set the tone; London's Carnaby Street became a place of pilgrimage for every fashion fan. In the 1970s, Italy began to raise its international fashion profile, with Italian stylists and designers appearing, more than anything, like fashion archeologists. No country is—or ever was—better at unearthing and highlighting other nations' treasures, and then marketing them as their own invention

(with a touch of Italian style). No one could be more British than the Italians, and they also recognized well ahead of the Americans the potential that lay in old US brands and classics. The Woolrich parka is a typical example of this: What was merely a functional garment in America became, thanks to Italian marketing, a cult object in Europe.

It really should be stressed that the Italians' search for inspiration from American and British fashions does not signify a lack of ideas. It is more a reflection of the yearning for the big, wide world—something common to many European countries after the Second World War. American fashion embodied, above all, a casual and youthful approach to fashion, combined with relaxed elegance.

Converses?
rock 'n' roll?

People were inspired by the fashions worn by off-duty, US soldiers in Italy, as well as by Hollywood films in the cinema. Not only did jeans and leisure shirts become part of everyday clothing in Europe but the canvas sneaker likewise acquired a new image. Rubber-soled, canvas shoes were invented in the mid-19th century for a variety of sporting activities. It was in the USA, however, that they first became popular as casual wear for children and young people and as weekend wear for adults. And in post-war Europe, US trends were widely copied by young people. Since the 1980s, Italian influence on many areas of fashion has grown steadily but US labels are still ahead in terms of mass-produced sportswear. And sometimes, a popular streetwear look can influence smart-casual wear.

Chuck Taylor All Star shoes by Converse, the name shortened to simply "Converses" or "Chucks," have become cult shoes for young people, even though they might prefer an elite sportswear brand like Polo Ralph Lauren or Timberland.

The canvas flat Superga shoe remains a fashionable alternative. During the 1980s, the yuppie decade, the Superga was very popular with youngsters and trendsetters of Italian leisure chic and was on a par with boat shoes, which were popu-lar at that time. In those days, Converses were reserved for streetwear. Superga was chic, whilst Converses were rock 'n' roll. Nowadays, such distinctions have become blurred and role models reversed. Converses are currently considered relatively decorous while Supergas are worn by those who like to shock.

Sneakers

Sneakers are the shoe equivalent of a T-Shirt. Anyone wearing sneakers feels fashionable, young, trendy, modern, and hip and embraces the principle of dressing for convenience. The notion of ironing shirts is as unfamiliar as polishing shoes. Hair is not combed, it is styled. Sneakers represent a type of lifestyle. Objectively, there is little to recommend most kinds of sneaker —they make your feet sweat, or fail to keep them warm. Vintage styles do not provide any shock absorption or foot support.

Despite the fact that sneakers have become a symbol of the modern, classless society, their history actually dates back to the 19th century. In those days, sneakers had flat soles made of natural rubber, and a light fabric upper, e.g. made of sailcloth. This type of shoe used to be worn for lawn sports, such as croquet. The first tennis shoes were invented during the early 20th century, otherwise sneakers were mainly familiar as cheap children's shoes. Sneakers began their rise to fame in the 1950s

as part of the new wave of youth fashion. At that time, leather shoes, e.g. penny loafers, cowboy, or motorcycle boots were in greater demand. It was not until the Seventies and Eighties that sneakers established themselves as anti-fashion footwear.

Nowadays, there is a confusing choice of sneakers on the market but they can still be divided into separate groups. On the one hand, we have the styles associated with the specific sports categories for which they were originally designed, e.g. the ankle-high styles originally associated with basketball and baseball, or bowling shoes with their thin leather soles. The uppers are mainly made from linen, synthetic fabric or leather, or, occasionally, real leather. There is also an exclusive range of sneakers made from high-grade materials and sometimes constructed by hand. Their design is based on sports shoes from the early 20th century, e.g. cycling shoes. However, most sneakers are the creation of shoe designers and have nothing whatsoever to do with sport.

Sturdy models

For many years, boots have occupied a shadowy role in the classic men's wardrobe. They have, at any rate, featured far less prominently than welt-stitched shoes or loafers, for example. Nevertheless, boots have been an integral part of a gentleman's wardrobe since its early beginnings in the early 18th century. To be precise, boots were once a gentleman's only real footwear and shoes were regarded for a while as a poor alternative. In fact, boots have always been appropriate footwear for a gentleman, and not just for riding purposes. The middle-classes imitated the style of the aristocratic gentleman but in the cities, more and more transport methods were being gradually introduced which no longer required the wearing of boots. As a result, boots became increasingly a feature of rural dress only.

Lace-up boots have a long history behind them. In their most familiar form, their origins date back to the footwear of the Blücher troops. Field marshal Blücher, born in 1742, lent his name to this open-laced shoe. Strictly speaking, the term "blucher" can only be applied to lace-up boots. Their advantage over traditional boots was presumably their lower price, since they were composed of several, smaller sections of leather. Typical examples of this type of boot are British hunting boots, as supplied by most Northampton boot and shoemakers. Alongside these models, which have a distinctly English profile thanks to their roots in hunting, American lace-up boots have a much more casual reputation. They were originally often seen in the form of footwear for workers or farmers, although the USA did also produce hunting boots. Hunting is considered a national sport throughout wide areas of North America and the clothing worn for this sport has little in the way of an elitist character.

Redwing boots are essentially work shoes, worn by farmers, mailmen, stable-boys, or carpenters. The fact that they are welt-stitched and made of solid leather has also made these shoes very popular in Europe—with people who are not normally involved with manual labor.

Thongs or flip flops

Sandals, whatever their style, have always been controversial. Those with straps or bands have a considerably longer tradition than the more modern European lace-up version. However, sandals are not recognized as proper footwear in any Western culture. Even in countries where sandals are accepted as everyday attire, businessmen are quick to discard them in favor of more classic shoes for encounters with Americans or Europeans.

Sandals offer the foot little protection, and thongs are sandals pared down even further. Not only are the materials reduced to a bare minimum but likewise the cost. Consequently, thongs are the normal footwear for most people in countries with tropical climates where they are very cheap to buy. In the Western world popular brands of thongs can cost almost as much as a proper shoe—an example of fashion madness taken to its extreme. Style connoisseurs turn their noses up at thongs—in their view, such footwear is simply uncivilized. Thongs do have their uses, however —on the beach, for example, or by the lakeside, in the countryside, in the yard, or perhaps even for a summertime shop-

ping expedition. Thongs should certainly not be dismissed out of hand any more than shorts or T-shirts.

1 Thongs require you to look after your feet. Make sure they look attractive before you even contemplate wearing a pair of thongs.

2 If you have to ask yourself whether thongs are too casual, the answer is inevitably "yes." They are always OK for the beach, by the swimming-pool, by the lakeside, in the garden, or in the fitness studio.

3 Thongs are comparable to tank tops: in other words, like a sleeveless shirt. If a tank top is suitable attire, then thongs will also be acceptable. In other words, virtually never.

4 Thongs should never be worn for anything that could be classed as a social event, and a shopping spree is considered such by many people.

5 Take care in Italy. Even if it is OK at home to wear thongs in summer, including to elegant fashion events, in Italy sandals of any kind will attract astonished looks even if worn for a stroll along the beach.

How a custom-made

The shoemaker begins by measuring the foot and taking an impression of the sole before an individual last is produced. Standard-sized lasts are used for ready-made shoes. (Photos: Eduard Meier).

The upper consists of several components, which are first cut out, then stitched together.

Upper leather and welt are sewn to the underside of the inner sole with a single seam.

Some shoemakers use wooden nails to attach the outer sole and heel to each other.

A pattern is imprinted in the welt, the ridge of leather which runs around the shoe.

A pattern is branded into the outside edge of the outer sole using a special branding iron.

shoe is made

The inner sole is hollowed out, leaving a raised edge around the perimeter, to which the welt and upper are attached.

The upper is stretched over the shank and is temporarily fixed to the last with nails.

The outer sole is stitched to the welt through pre-punched holes using linen thread.

The edge of the sole is trimmed or filed, then sealed and polished with shoe polish and cream.

A bone is used to polish the shoe to a shiny finish. Any uneven surfaces will be smoothed out at the same time.

Finally, wax polish and water is used to give the leather a high-gloss patina.

A glossary

Blucher is a shoe with open lacing.

Box calf is calfskin taken from very young animals.

Brogue is a shoe which is decorated with tiny, perforated holes.

Budapest is the Hungarian version of a brogue.

Cordovan is horsehide. This used to be widely available but has become increasingly expensive as automobiles and tractors have replaced the horse.

Custom-made shoe is a term used for any shoe which is constructed according to an individually produced last.

Derby is a shoe with open lacing. The recommended choice for men with a high instep as it molds itself easily to the individual foot shape. However, the Derby is considered a less formal shoe.

Goodyear is the name of the man who invented the machinery for sewing uppers and welts together in a process that was much quicker than by hand. Good quality shoes from the USA or Great Britain often have this name imprinted on the outer soles as a mark of quality.

Hand-stitched shoes are those in which the upper and welt are sewn together by hand. Shoe enthusiasts argue as to whether the machine-finished Goodyear shoe is inferior to the hand-stitched product or not. The factory-produced shoe is regarded as easier to repair because the insole lip (cf. separate entry) is glued in place.

Hand-sewn are any decorative seams in hand-produced shoes; otherwise the stitching is done by machine.

Inner sole is the inside sole of a shoe on which the foot rests.

Insole lip or rib The insole lip is a strip of leather attached to the underside of the inner sole with adhesive tape. The welt and upper are stitched to the insole lip. On a custom-made shoe, the insole lip is usually carved out of the inner sole using a special knife.

Last reproduces the shape of the foot, around which the shoe is constructed.

Loafer has a more sophisticated ring to it than "moccasin" or "slip-on shoe".

Longwing is a wingtip shoe in which the toecap extends right back to the heel.

Made-to-measure signifies a personal order, whereby the client can choose a particular type of shoe in his own choice of leather.

Manufacturer is the term for the factory in which welt-stitched shoes are made. Despite

# of shoe terms

the machinery, some hand-stitching is still required.

Monk straps are shoes which fasten with a buckle.

Oxford is a shoe with closed lacing and a straight toecap.

Penny loafer is so-called from the custom of putting a coin under the cross-strap of the shoe for luck.

Plaintip is a shoe, the front of which is made from a single piece of leather with no need for a separate toecap. Plaintips are considered more formal than Oxfords.

Slip-on shoes or slip-ons are an alternative name for loafers.

Slipper is a type of shoe only worn indoors.

Suede is the more common term for raw hide.

Tassel loafers are loafers with little tassels.

Welt-stitched shoes have three advantages: the shoe is stable but remains flexible, the sole can be completely renewed, and the cork filler and inner sole will mold themselves to the exact shape of the foot.

Wingtip is a backwards-extending toecap.

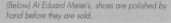

(Below) At Eduard Meier's, shoes are polished by hand before they are sold.

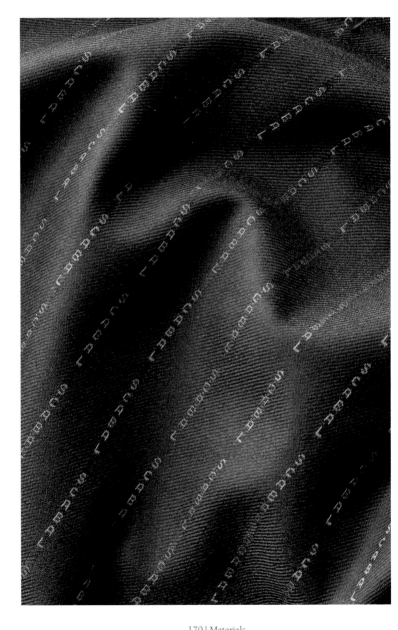

How to buy efficiently

Usually, no one likes buying something without giving it much thought, but that is precisely what most men do when they purchase clothes, shoes, or accessories—often paying out considerable sums of money into the bargain. This is not quite so bad if the clothing in question happens to be leisurewear, as any mistakes would only damage the ill-advised shopper's wallet. However, if he is buying a suit to wear for work, such a poor choice might have far-reaching consequences. An excessively expensive suit in the wrong color, which may not even fit properly, could seriously damage the image of its wearer—quite apart from the heavy financial loss incurred.

When men are about to buy something new, they usually proceed very methodically, researching prices, quality, various makes, and, equally importantly, what service they can expect from the product. Only when they are thoroughly familiar with the market and what is available will they reach a final decision. Very sensibly, they will go to the same trouble even in the case of relatively inexpensive items. Their approach is very different, however, when it comes to clothes. A man will happily spend 600 dollars or more purchasing a suit on impulse, with no preparation and often while pressed for time. The same is also true of neckties, shoes, or shirts. The reason why there is such a contrast in the amounts of time spent on planning and buying is self-evident. Men are not particularly interested in what they wear. The majority are much happier buying entertainment technology, electrical gadgets, tools, sports equipment, or watches.

Nonetheless, anyone willing to spend a little time finding out about the different materials, manufacturing methods, price ranges, and quality indicators relating to clothes and accessories is certain to get far more pleasure out of a shopping trip, not to mention from wearing and using the purchases. Some men actually find that their research sparks a deeper interest in the subject and they end up viewing fashion as something of a hobby, in which case the pleasure is guaranteed.

Anyone with fashion know-how can dream up imaginative ideas of his own, such as having his name woven into stripes by Scabal, the Belgian cloth merchants.

Fabrics: the basics

In days when cloth was still spun and woven, cut out and stitched, darned and patched at home, children automatically absorbed some basic knowledge of the subject of textiles. It is rare nowadays for clothes to be made at home. They are merely purchased without being understood. Here, therefore, is a brief, condensed summary of basic facts about textile weaving.

Fabrics are essentially made from animal- or plant-based fibers. The most common animal fiber is sheep hair while the most familiar, modern, plant fiber is cotton. Since we are only concerned here with basic principles, let us concentrate our full attention on the king of fibers: sheep's wool. After the sheep is shorn, the worst of the dirt is removed from its curly, woolly fleece. The wool is then washed and, finally, combed for as long as it takes to turn it into long strands. These are stretched further and further until only the longest fibers remain. These are then spun into thread by twisting the strands.

A set of threads, known as the warp, is held lengthwise under tension on a rectangular frame, or loom. More threads, known as the weft, are then interlaced laterally through these longitudinal threads at right-angles to them. In order to produce a cohesive whole, the lateral threads, or weft, are inserted first over, and then under the warp thread, thereby creating the weave, or fabric.

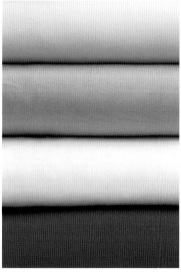

Clearly the fabric can only be as strong as the threads of which it is made. In order to make a stronger cloth, several threads can be twisted together prior to weaving. The resulting thread is called twist yarn. Both the warp and weft can consist of twist yarn, but if only one or the other consists of twisted yarn, the result is known as either a warp- or weft-twist fabric. High-twist yarn consists of a relatively high number of twists per inch. Twisted yarn often consists of more than one type of fiber, e.g. polyester and cotton.

The woven fabric is then washed in soapy water and dried. Any projecting fiber ends are burned off before it is pressed flat with a large hot rotary iron. The result is called a worsted fabric, from which the short fibers have been removed by combing, leaving only long fibers. The short fibers, which have been combed out, are also spun into yarn. This is not as smooth as the yarn spun from long fibers, since the short fibers stick out everywhere. This type of yarn is used for woolen fabrics such as tweed. Woolen materials are the best option for suits, sports jackets, and coats. Cotton-based fabrics are a popular choice for pants as they feel pleasanter in direct contact with the skin. Typical cotton fabrics used for pants include cord, moleskin, twill weaves and, of course, denim for casual wear. For a long time, the most important plant-based fabric in Europe was linen, since cotton did not arrive until it was brought from the colonies. Silk is an animal fiber, and is mainly used for the accessories in a gentleman's wardrobe.

All fabrics shown are by COVE & CO.

Fabrics for suits

Cotton is very pleasant to wear, especially in summer. However, it quickly loses its shape, and crumples and creases easily. Anyone who does not mind this happening will be very happy with a suit made from this vegetable fiber.

Cotton and synthetics Synthetics are scorned by fans of hand-made clothing. However, as with woolen materials, the addition of synthetic fibers to cotton helps the suit to keep its shape in hot, humid climates.

Linen is made from the fibers of the flax plant. It has a reputation for creasing, a tendency which, in higher-quality fabrics, lessens over the course of time. Once the creases have finally dropped out, the look of linen is unmistakable.

Cashmere is considered the ultimate luxury fabric. The best quality fabrics come from Mongolia. Unlike sheep's wool, the soft, bottom hair of the cashmere goat is not shorn, but instead is collected up, or carefully combed out.

Silk did not find its way back into gentlemen's tailoring until after the Second World War. It was initially used for evening wear but eventually began to be used in suits and sports jackets.

Vicuña wool is a fabric woven from the hair of a South American camelid, a relative of the llama. The vicuña population is very small, which makes the raw material extremely rare and very difficult to obtain. Its wool can consequently be astronomically expensive.

Wool has been used for suits for hundreds of years. To this day, there really is no other material for suits, pants, or coats that can compete with wool in terms of shape retention, elasticity, and durability.

Gregor and Peter Thissen, who own the company Scabal, introduced the world's first worsted spun vicuña in 1980.

Wool and synthetics A small amount of synthetic yarn can help lightweight woolen fabrics retain their shape. This is only really necessary in hot, humid climates: In other parts of the world, mixed fabrics of this type are rarely used.

Wool and silk Wool and silk threads can be mixed to various effects. Sometimes the silk content is only present in an ornamental seam—for example, in a plaid, latticework pattern. In other cases, it influences the character of the entire cloth.

Pure luxury: cashmere & co.

PURE UNDERSTATEMENT—ONLY THE TAILOR AND HIS CLIENT KNOW THE VALUE OF THE FABRIC

Cashmere and vicuña (see above) are considered the ultimate in exclusivity. The former comes from the coat of the cashmere goat while the other is made from the hair of a small llama, native to the Andes. Both animals produce extremely fine fibers, which, in the case of cashmere, is not obtained by shearing but from laboriously collecting clumps of hair in the wild. In spring, cashmere goats shed some of their coat. Shepherds collect the fibers that have caught on bushes and rocks. The goats cannot be shorn or else the animals would freeze to death. Such consideration was not given to the vicuña in times past and, up until the 1950s, this animal was quite simply shot and killed for its coat, which almost led to its extinction. From the mid-1970s, any trade in vicuña wool was banned for 20 years but was legalized again in the mid-1990s. Anyone who wants to indulge in something really special can commission his tailor to make him a coat of vicuña wool, provided he is willing to part with between 20,000 and 25,000 dollars.

Spinning and weaving

Yarn is the keyboard, or scale of notes, from which a textile designer composes his fabrics. The weaving methods introduce the harmonies, while the graph paper, on which the weave is recorded, is the equivalent of the score. It is true to say that the work which goes on in the design department of a weaving mill does indeed resemble that of a composer. Just as a musician can put different sounds together in a passage of music to create a particular harmony, in the same way a textile designer can select different colored threads and arrange them lengthways and crossways into a specific design.

Prior to the weaving process, warp threads, i.e. the longitudinal threads, are interlaced and held taut in a rectangular frame. Lateral threads—known as weft threads—are then interlaced to transform the parallel but unconnected warp threads into a cohesive weave. The characteristics of a weave emerge when the weft is inserted first over, then under the warp thread and is consequently alternately visible on the right and wrong sides of the finished fabric. Designs emerge as the weft is woven in a regular, recurring pattern between the warp threads, resulting in a particular type of weave.

The task of the designer is to decide on the appearance of the fabric by determining the type of weave and the colors to be used. He will design the weave on paper

The designers at cloth manufacturing firms, such as the Italian firm Zegna, dictate fashion with their collections.

or on his computer screen. It is usually done in black and white to begin with and is only colored in at a later stage. He can choose from a palette of colors in the form of sample yarns supplied for design purposes by the spinning mills in a multitude of different shades.

Just as different colors are mixed into the yarn, the weave also comprises different, colored threads. Even a single-color cloth, e.g. in dark blue, will not necessarily be woven exclusively from dark-blue warp and weft threads. This mixing of colors is also responsible for the fact that an apparently single-color material can suddenly develop a reddish, or greenish, or violet shimmer when viewed in a certain light—an interesting effect which does not occur in fabrics that are dyed in one procedure (in other words, after they are woven). Sometimes, different yarns are combined. For example, a warp thread, which is eventually intended to form a pin stripe, may consist of a silk yarn whereas the rest of the threads may consist of wool.

To get a better idea of the proposed fabric, a sample of the cloth is woven. This design template is known as *Schablone* in German and *tableau* in French. After careful examination, the most successful variations are cut out and these small samples are then glued or attached to cards. The collection is then presented to the client, and if a sufficient number of orders is placed subsequently for one or another of the designs, then weaving can begin.

The yarn is the basis of the cloth. It is spun from the fibers of different types of animal hair.

Under the microscope: quality control

When it is first woven, the fabric—which will eventually arrive in cloth merchants' storerooms and on the tailor's cutting table as a silky soft and expensively shimmering luxury weave—feels and looks more like a robust cleaning cloth, and is initially treated with a corresponding lack of respect. The feather-light, Super 200 cashmere lies in a crumpled heap on the floor, awaiting an expert to check it for possible flaws.

After an initial examination, the cloth is then sent to the control department where minute flaws, barely visible with the naked eye, are found and removed. Utter silence and concentration reign in the work rooms. Equipped with special magnifying spectacles, highly trained women—experience has shown that men are not suited to this level of precision work—slowly examine the roll of material a centimeter at a time and make a note of any tiny faults, such as torn threads or small knots in the yarn.

Spotting these tiny irregularities is an art in itself, and elimi-nating them verges on magic: using an extremely fine needle, the faulty areas are replaced by hand, thread by thread—in other words, rewoven. The term "invisible mending" does perfectly describe

Cloth is woven from warp and weft, interlaced according to a particular rhythm.

the most extraordinary skill practiced in this department.

Tailors also resort to this seemingly magic ability to make faults simply disappear—for example, when a customer accidentally burns a hole in his suit. Most weaving mills only accept such tasks when the damaged garment is from their own manufacture, but when this is indeed the case, the singed area is rewoven using original threads, complete with warp and weft. The needles used to perform this and other miracles are personally distributed to each seamstress by the manager of the workshop at the beginning of each and every working day.

These fine precision tools are then collected in again and meticulously counted

each evening. If a needle does ever happen to go missing, it needs to be established beyond reasonable doubt that it has not been left in the material itself—the damage that such a foreign body could cause later would be too great to contemplate.

High-grade fabrics at Zegna being meticulously checked for flaws after weaving.

Finishing: the fabric is completed

Once the weaving specialists have done all they can to remove even the tiniest flaws in the fabric, the cloth is transported to a processing plant that handles the finishing. The first step is to wash the material in giant drums of water and soap. This procedure helps to remove any particles of dirt which the fabric has inevitably absorbed during the spinning, weaving, and checking stages, and, at the same time, it also helps to soften the fabric. The degree of softness required is decided by the client, i.e. the weaving firm, but since softness is a relative concept, the result will largely depend on the touch and the experience of the finisher. He has to be able to achieve the desired effect by accurately judging the duration of the washing cycle. In other words, he must know whether the Super 120 cashmere with a weight of 230 grams needs ten minutes' washing or twelve, or even 20. In most cases, this calculation can only be made by a human being and not by a computer. The relatively few experts in this field play a key role in the weaving houses—one wrong decision and a fabric could be ruined. Conversely, a well-judged addition at the right

After wet finishing, the surface of the fabric is then brushed with thistles.

moment can turn a good product into an absolutely outstanding one.

After the washing process, the lengths of fabric are placed in large spinning machines, then carefully dried by passing them over heated rollers in a type of hot mangle which stretches the fabric at the same time. Singeing follows next, which involves burning off any projecting fiber ends. For the shearing process, the fabric is placed in rotating drums, fitted with blades, which operate much like rotary lawn mowers. The so-called decating process begins by removing any shine which may have been caused by the mangle procedure, and then proceeds to give the fabric a new lustrous finish. Between stages, the fabric is repeatedly steamed, stretched, and pressed. Finally, the entire length of fabric is laid by hand between 1,000 or so cardboard sheets, every tenth one of which is heated.

The fabric in this pile is subjected to around 2,000 psi of pressure (about 150 bar). This labor-intensive process gives the fabric the sort of high-quality sheen that will guarantee its popularity with both the tailor and his client.

After a production process lasting at least five weeks, the finished fabric is returned to the weaving house, and placed in the warehouse to await dispatch to the cloth merchants or to be sent directly to custom tailoring establishments or ready-to-wear factories. The finished garment is proof in itself that all the effort involved in this process is worthwhile.

The finishing process produces the desired "hand," or feel in a fabric and gives it a high-quality luster.

What do we mean by "hand-made?"

Since the 18th century, machines and technology have been an integral part of the fashion industry. To do without them completely would mean turning the clock back 200 years. Nevertheless, it is considered highly prestigious for one's suit, shirts, neckties, or shoes to carry a "hand-made"—or *fatto a mano*—label, guaranteeing the wearer admittance to the VIP lounge of top-end fashion. Is there any justification for this or are we merely paying the price of nostalgia? Is a bespoke suit really better than one which is factory-made? Do hand-stitched shoes last longer? And what exactly does "hand-made" mean anyway? A comparison of hand-made and machine-produced items will undoubtedly produce the answers to these questions.

THE SUIT What are we supposed to think when a suit label states "hand tailored?" Did a tailor sew the entire ensemble with a needle and thread? Yes and no, since no work is carried out completely without a machine nowadays. "Hand-made," therefore, means that the cutting pattern is marked out on the fabric by hand (not by cutting plotter), the individual sections are cut out with a pair of shears (and not using a computer-aided electronic blade or laser), tacked together with a needle and thread, stitched together using a sewing-machine or by hand, and, every now and again, they are pressed into shape and smoothed

A tailor-made, hand-stitched suit represents more than 60 hours of work. The above photo shows the London "bespoke" tailor, John Coggin, sewing in a lining.

using an iron. A tailor will reach for his needle for three reasons: firstly, if a particularly flexible or pliable seam is required, for example around the shoulder or the seat (a machine-sewn seam will split open if it is over-strained). Secondly, in order to add decorative hand stitching, for instance along the front edges, the breast pocket, or the side seams. Thirdly, in situations where a machine cannot perfectly replicate a hand-sewn task, such as a hand-stitched buttonhole.

Hand-sewn versus machine-sewn: The fabric can be sewn together in such a way that the pattern or stripes in the finished product flow uninterruptedly across the seams. The garment will fit the wearer better if certain sections are sewn by hand. The fabric can be shaped around the anatomy more accurately by hand-pressing. Buttonholes can be stitched far more elegantly and a few slightly irregular, hand stitches will merely serve to add a touch of distinction to the completed garment.

Machine-sewn versus hand-sewn: A client's measurements can be converted into a cutting pattern in a matter of seconds with the aid of a computer and plotter. Single-color fabrics are cut out faster and more accurately by machine. A machine can work more quickly and just as efficiently, if not better, when it comes to tasks such as the time-consuming basting of interfacings. Where straight stitching is required, a machine produces a more even result, e.g. in the case of pants' side seams. An automatic press can carry out some types of pressing procedures better than a tailor with a hot iron.

Which is the better suit? A hand-made suit is more comfortable to wear and should sit better (provided it fits properly). For any other criteria, the advantages of a hand-made suit are more a matter of aesthetics and an emotional preference.

SHIRTS Nowadays, hand-made shirts are increasingly only found in Italy. A *cucito a mano* (hand-sewn) or *fatto a mano* (hand-made) label means that the material was cut out by hand, the sleeves were sewn

At Emanuel Berg, the custom shirtmakers, made-to-order shirts are cut out by hand.

into the body of the shirt by hand, and the shoulder seams, collar, buttonhole panel, sleeve vents, buttonholes, and triangular gussets on the underarms were all hand-stitched. It is very rare for the buttons to be entirely attached by hand: Generally speaking, this is mostly done by machine, leaving a seamstress to sew in the threads at the end.

Hand-sewn versus machine-sewn: The fit is more precise, stripes and checked patterns run uninterruptedly across the seams, breast pocket and sleeve vents. The more flexible hand-stitched seam can make the shirt more comfortable to wear as it contains a small amount of give, thereby molding itself better to the body. Hand-sewn buttonholes are very distinctive and, what is more, they do not fray.

The seam of a hand-stitched necktie (Ascot) is more elastic and flexible.

Machine-sewn versus hand-sewn: If operated by specialist staff, a machine can sew very accurate and extremely durable seams. Time-saving production methods are reflected in lower prices. Machined buttonholes are softer and easier to fasten.

Which is the better shirt? Any shirt that is carefully made from a good fabric will be a good shirt, regardless of whether it was sewn by hand or machine. Fans of handmade shirts will be charmed by the slightly irregular appearance of the hand stitching and the specific shape of the sleeve, but whether these are objective advantages is something you will have to decide.

NECKTIE There are three ways of making neckties. The simplest method is to sew together a tube of material on an ordinary sewing-machine. The disadvantage of this is that the seam, which consists of an upper and lower thread, is not flexible and the necktie can be difficult to tie. The second method uses a Liba machine, which sews with a single thread, and necessitates the tie being turned inside out (then turned right side out again afterwards). The third

method involves hand stitching. The necktie is cut out by hand, laid in position, fixed together with pins, and then sewn with a needle and thread.

Hand-sewn versus machine-sewn: Any design patterns (e.g. diamond shapes or dots) are cut to run symmetrically toward the point, stripes end along the edge. The interfacing fits exactly into the tube of fabric as the tie is sewn right side out and nothing can slip. After the necktie is sewn up, the residual length of thread is not sewn in but left in reserve. When the tie is knotted, the fabric retains a little bit of movement back and forth on the thread. This saves wear on the material and makes it easier to knot.

Machine-sewn versus hand-sewn: This is the more time-saving option, as a machine can sew a necktie together in a few seconds. No fluctuations in terms of quality occur, since a machine's stitching never varies—unlike humans, it is not susceptible to moods or physical ailments.

Which is the better necktie? The way a necktie is made is only half the story—of equal importance is the quality of the fabric; in other words, whether it is silk, cashmere, wool, or linen, etc. The best type of necktie, therefore, is one which is carefully made by hand from top-quality material.

SHOES One hundred percent hand-made shoes are extremely rare since even the most exclusive makers of custom-made shoes, after cutting out the individual parts of the upper leather by hand, use a sewing machine to stitch them together (except for moccasins, which have a hand-stitched vamp and decorative stitching on the upper). The rest of the task should then be completed in the workshop using an awl (for piercing guide holes in the leather), a needle, thread, blades, files, and various other specialist tools. Otherwise, the shoes could not be classed as genuinely hand-made but industrially produced.

Hand-stitched versus machine-stitched: A hand-stitched shoe is more solid, as the connecting seam goes right through the upper leather, the inner sole, and the welt. Here is a brief explanation of how welt-stitched shoes are made: In a factory-made shoe, in order to be able to sew the upper, welt, and inner sole together, a narrow strip of leather, known as the insole rib, or lip, is attached to the inner sole with a strip of adhesive tape. The seam which holds the shoe together (invisible in a ready-made shoe) goes through the insole lip. A shoe-maker, on the other hand, does not glue an insole lip in place but, instead, carves out the inner sole from underneath, leaving a ridge around the edge, to which the upper and welt can be attached. The sole seam is embedded in a narrow groove, which makes it invisible as well as protecting it. Hand-made shoes are easier to repair, as the needle can be inserted through the original holes in the welt and inner sole.

Machine-stitched versus hand-stitched: Time-saving, e.g. in shoes with sewn soles. The upper is mechanically pulled over the last and pressed into shape, which takes mere seconds. Stitching the shaft, inner sole, and welt together is a faster procedure with a Goodyear machine, as is stitching the outer sole and welt together.

Which is the better shoe? If two pairs of shoes with sewn soles were made from the same last from the same leather, one by machine and one by hand, the resulting shoes would be virtually identical in terms of appearance and comfort. They would even be the same in terms of durability, provided they were cared for correctly.

To sum up: Hand-made products are usually more attractive and, sometimes, the better product, objectively speaking—but only if the work is flawless and the design lives up to the highest standards. If the craftsman has no sense of taste or style, or finds himself technically challenged, the end result will not be up to much. It is sometimes difficult to distinguish the dividing line between hand-made and machine-made since virtually every machine used in the fashion industry is operated by specialist staff.

The sole edge of an Eduard Meier custom-made shoe is sealed with a hot iron.

Spend to save

Politicians continually rack their brains over how to encourage people to overcome their unwillingness to consume. A tried and true method of getting more people into stores comes in the form of reduced price sales. Low prices attract buyers like a magnet, thereby keeping customer numbers up and guaranteeing increased turnover. Even people who are otherwise careful about budgeting suddenly abandon all restraint at the sight of bargain prices. The more drastically the high prices of coveted labels are slashed, the more ruthless they become. Acquiring a 25-dollar sweater at half price produces far less satisfaction than a 50 percent-reduction on a purse costing 2,500 dollars. Rightly so—since goods which started off cheap do not get any better as a result of a price reduction. Conversely, quality clothing does not become worse, just more obtainable. Astute consumers know this and delay their shopping spree until the end-of-season sales. Why pay 2,000 dollars for a suit in October, when two months later it can, with a bit of luck, be bought for half that amount?

In many countries, sales have been something of a cult for decades and for well-heeled customers, especially, they are an integral part of their consumption planning. The English gentleman may well have his suits made by a "bespoke" tailor but he will pick up his neckties and sweaters in the "sales." To this day, elegant London society still speaks nostalgically of the "one-day sales" which used to be held by Turnbull & Asser, the Jermyn Street gentleman's outfitters and shirtmakers—even though the last of these was held in 1980. As far as gossip columnist and Princess Margaret biographer Nigel Dempster was concerned, it was as much a part of the social calendar as Ascot or Wimbledon, but even more rewarding. A similar fashion legend in Germany is Eduard Meier in Munich, Germany's oldest shoemakers. Peter-Eduard Meier, who is now the 13th generation to run the family firm (with his sister Brigitte), points out, not without a degree of pride, that even well-known travel companies highlight the store's "special sale." The company, former purveyor to the Bavarian royal court, prefers to avoid using the term "clearance sale" to describe its twice-yearly reduction in shoe and clothing prices: "We turn the store completely into a discount outlet, limit personal advice to ensuring the right size and, in this way, provide a large number of people with the opportunity to sample our high-quality stock. Many of them acquire a taste for it and return to make other purchases during the season itself."

Assembling a complete wardrobe from bargains takes considerable patience. Classics, such as dark-blue sports jackets, gray suits, or black Oxfords are rarely reduced in price and even if they are, you are unlikely to find anything in your size in a sale. However, if you know of a good tailoring alteration service, the odds of getting a bargain increase accordingly. But the cost of any alteration must be reasonable when compared to the savings made in the sale. One rule of thumb holds that any alterations should not cost more than 20 percent of the regular price. Clearly, altering a reduced item works out relatively expensive but often is well worth it. The following example illustrates this: A suit that normally costs 2,000 dollars is reduced to 999 dollars in the sale. If you invest 20 per cent of the normal price (20 per cent of 2,000 dollars equals 400 dollars) in having it altered, you will end up with a well-fitting suit for a total of 1,399 dollars (701 dollars less than its normal cost). It is worth doing the sums.

Buying tips

1 Bargain prices are very tempting. Always consider whether you are tempted by the amount you will save or the product itself. Would it still be as attractive at its original price?

2 It is sometimes difficult to remain rational when faced with big reductions. Think before buying a garment about whether it will go with the rest of your wardrobe and will meet all your quality criteria.

3 Be aware that sales staff may try to pressure you, so do not succumb to it. It may indeed be true that there is only one item of its kind left in the store but you should still be permitted time to think about your purchase before buying. So, leave the store and have a quiet think about it outside.

4 A relatively drastic reduction can sometimes fool you into believing that the sale price, which may still be pitched quite high, is a better deal than it is. Check carefully that the bargain price is not still too high, e.g. in the case of shoes with sewn soles costing "only" 500 instead of 900 dollars.

5 It may be advisable to take a friend with you when you go shopping. This may deter you from getting swept up into a dangerous buying frenzy. Although critical comments may be irritating at the time, you may be grateful later on.

6 If you regret a purchase, you will have to rely on the store's good will. You are not automatically entitled to an exchange unless the product is faulty. Remedying your shopping mistakes can be difficult. You do not normally get much of a return by selling them on eBay.

7 If you know very well that you are a person who finds it difficult to resist the temptations of the sales, you should avoid going shopping in the first place. It takes a great deal of willpower to resist buying something already in your hand. Staying at home, on the other hand, is relatively easy.

ACCESSORIES OFTEN HAVE A GREATER IMPACT THAN
CLOTHES AND SHOULD BE CHOSEN WITH EXTRA CARE.

Accessories

What would happen if the President stepped up to the podium one morning with his nose pierced? The media would not be able to resist commenting on that tiny piece of ornamentation. When it comes to appearance, small things often have a significant impact. The item in question may be nothing more than a necktie motif, which is only discernible close to, a cuff link, a discreet ankle tattoo, or a ring.

In the world of fashion, such minor additions to our clothing are called "accessories." Some of them, for example, purses or belts, may not be all that minor but what they do have in common is that they make all the difference to the total look. A yellow leather strap on a classic wristwatch cannot fail to attract attention. So, although you do not always have to do very much to create an impact, it is important to know exactly what you are doing—like a chef who knows precisely the right amount of each spice to use.

Jewelry is likewise classed as an "accessory." Many men have long considered it perfectly normal to adorn themselves with bracelets, earrings, finger rings, chains around the neck, and even hair bands. Business or formal wear, however, demands a more restrained approach to this kind of ornamentation. What might be admired on a football celebrity or a rock musician might be frowned upon if worn by an ordinary member of the public.

If you want to play it safe, stick to a wristwatch, wedding ring, possibly one other ring, and cuff links. Anything more might be viewed as excessive—at least if worn with a business outfit. Jewelry is regarded as distracting. People are also quick to disapprove of accessories that are overly trendy. Better to leave your fashionable sunglasses in their case.

With the role of accessories steadily growing in importance in recent years, famous firms like Belvest now present their collections complete with matching accessories.

FAQs on belts

COLOR Belts should match your shoes. Black shoes require a black belt, brown shoes, a brown belt. Brown tones should be coordinated according to the respective shade (i.e. chocolate brown, reddish brown, burgundy, cognac, etc.) and/or color lightness (i.e. light brown with light brown, medium brown with medium brown, etc.). In the case of casual, fabric belts (cf. chapter on "Materials"), the color should be dictated by any leather elements in the outfit.

MATERIAL Leather belts only with a business suit or combination (e.g. blazer or tweed jacket with flannel pants). Braided belts are also acceptable with casual or summer suits, and fabric (e.g. striped canvas) can be worn with sporty pants (e.g. chinos or jeans). Caution: the "Real Leather" tag can also apply to cheap, split leather and is sometimes misleadingly used on belts made of reconstituted leather (the equivalent of chipboard compared to solid wood). High-quality retailers would not stock such products, however.

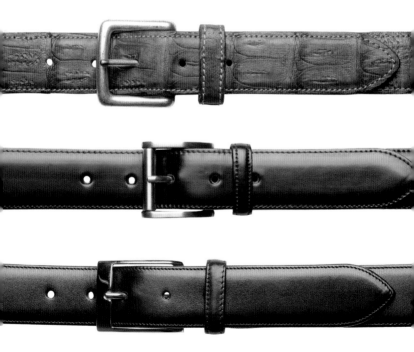

LENGTH, WIDTH, AND THICKNESS
Most belts have five holes. Ideally, (and prior to a business lunch) the buckle prong would go through the middle, or third, hole. The rule with regard to width and thickness is: narrow and thin = formal, wide and thick = casual. Belts for dark suits should measure 1–1.25 inches (2.5–3.5 cm), casual styles about 1.5 inches (4 cm).

BUCKLE The color of the belt buckle (solid brass or sterling silver) must match any metal in your watch, jewelry, or accessories. A gold-colored brass buckle should be worn with gold cuff links and watch, a silver, buckled belt with a stainless steel chronometer watch and white-gold or plati-num cuff links. A belt buckle must also match the buckles on monk strap shoes. The rule on design and size is: the more subtle and delicate the design, the more formal the effect. Buckles carrying logos or motifs should be worn with caution.

When should a belt be worn and when not? With any suit (although purists prefer suspenders with a double-breasted suit or vest). Belts are taboo with tails or morning dress (a gentleman would wear suspenders with either of these), but have become widely accepted with a tuxedo.

Examples of belts made by Kreis of Obertshausen in Germany.

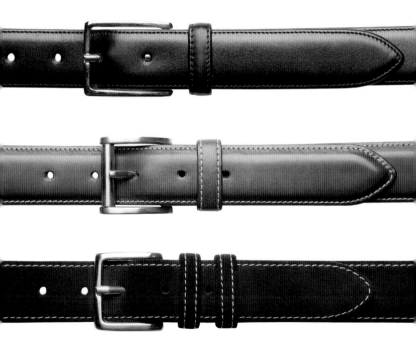

Socks

Knee-length socks are the best option with a dark business suit, providing a solid background linking your shoes and pants. Calf-length socks are fine with narrow-cut trousers as closer fitting pants do not ride up as easily. Whatever the length of the socks, they should be a dark color, e.g. black, dark gray, or navy blue.

In America, discreetly patterned socks are the ultimate as style items. Wall Street

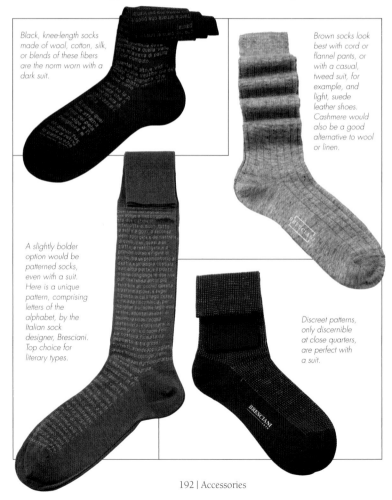

Black, knee-length socks made of wool, cotton, silk, or blends of these fibers are the norm worn with a dark suit.

Brown socks look best with cord or flannel pants, or with a casual, tweed suit, for example, and light, suede leather shoes. Cashmere would also be a good alternative to wool or linen.

A slightly bolder option would be patterned socks, even with a suit. Here is a unique pattern, comprising letters of the alphabet, by the Italian sock designer, Bresciani. Top choice for literary types.

Discreet patterns, only discernible at close quarters, are perfect with a suit.

brokers often favor a herringbone pattern or black-and-white Glen plaid with their dark-gray, chalk-striped suits. Longitudinal, two-tone stripes are also considered to be elegant. An example well worth emulating!

British men, however, have always had a penchant for bold colors around the ankles. Red, pink, yellow, or bright green are all typical sock colors for some London businessmen in pinstripe, navy suits. But brightly colored socks are considered inappropriate for business wear in Germany. Any German wishing to try this style would have to possess a fair amount of fashion nerve—and not be fazed by caustic remarks.

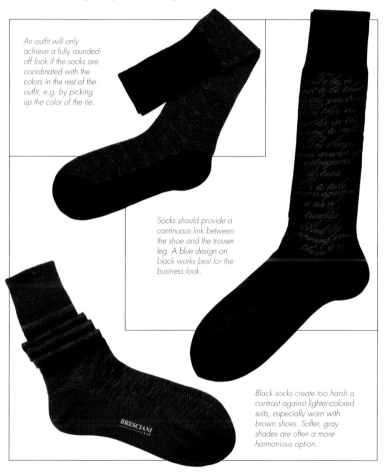

An outfit will only achieve a fully rounded-off look if the socks are coordinated with the colors in the rest of the outfit, e.g. by picking up the color of the tie.

Socks should provide a continuous link between the shoe and the trouser leg. A blue design on black works best for the business look.

Black socks create too harsh a contrast against lighter-colored suits, especially worn with brown shoes. Softer, gray shades are often a more harmonious option.

What socks are made of

CLASSIC WOOL: Socks made from sheep's hair create the perfect environment for one's feet. Woolen fibers keep the foot warm and are a natural deodorant, which is why wool socks can be worn at all times of the year—fine wool ones in summer and thicker ones in cold weather. Synthetic fibers are sometimes added to wool to improve the fit and help the socks keep their shape. Objectively speaking, this does not alter the qualities of wool.

COOL COTTON: For many men, cotton is the favorite sock material of all, familiar to them from their sports socks. Cotton does, indeed, feel cool on the skin, which is why summer socks are frequently made of it. Cotton socks have the disadvantage

however, that feet cool down more quickly in cotton than wool.

ELEGANT SILK: Silk socks were always a mark of elegance and exclusivity. Nowadays, they are mainly worn with evening wear. However, silk is often blended with wool, creating a material that is eminently suitable for wearing with business attire.

LUXURIOUS CASHMERE: Cashmere, like silk, is the epitome of luxury. Since it is impossible to tell a cashmere sock from a wool or cotton sock just by looking at it, it also represents the epitome of understatement. Even men who normally dislike receiving socks as presents cannot fail to be delighted with a gift of this type of sock, which is why they are very much in demand before Christmas.

The correct way to wash socks

THE MORE DELICATE THE SOCK, THE GENTLER THE TREATMENT IT REQUIRES.

NATURAL-FIBER SOCKS Follow the care instructions carefully: They will show the correct washing temperature. For hygiene reasons, socks should be turned inside out before washing. If in any doubt as to which is the right program, always choose a setting for delicate fabrics and use a mild detergent. Generally speaking, a dryer should not cause any damage but it would be safer, even so, to leave the socks to dry in the fresh air. Although hanging socks out to dry takes time and occupies space, it does prevent accidents. Luxury silk or cashmere socks are best washed by hand and should, as a rule, avoid contact with the dryer—they belong unequivocally on the washing-line.

SPORTS AND EXERCISE SOCKS Cotton or mixed-fiber sports socks should be washed at 104 °F/40 °C. Functional fabrics should be washed using a special detergent, guaranteed to preserve the specific properties of the fibers. Carefully follow the instructions on the label. Sports socks can normally be dried in the dryer.

Do not look into my eyes

Once upon a time, sunglasses were merely worn as a protection against dazzling light—for example, by pilots, mountain hikers, or automobile drivers. Nowadays, sunglasses function primarily as an accessory. Although they are, of course, still worn to protect the eyes from bright sunlight, they have become, first and foremost, a symbol of style—a state of affairs illustrated by the fact that there is no longer a convincing correlation between sunshine and the wearing of sunglasses. Am I exaggerating? Well, only a little. Dark glasses are predominantly selected on the basis of style criteria and purchased like clothes or other accessories. Some people always buy the latest

Narrow glasses which are slightly curved provide the eyes with all-round protection from glare.

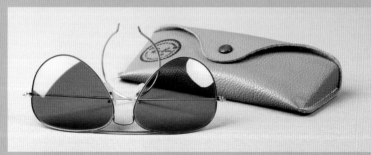

Pilots' sunglasses with sports-style frames, reminiscent of the 1980s, contain heavier lenses.

model, the one that has just been hyped up by advertising and PR publicity, while others stick to classic favorites, most of which originate in the USA, the birthplace of sunglasses as an accessory.

Sunglasses' dark lenses protect the wearer from dazzling light and harmful UV rays, as well as from intrusive stares. Wide frames shield the eyes at the sides and a flat rim covers the eyebrows and the areas either side of the nose. Extra large glasses are therefore very popular if you want to preserve your anonymity and hide your emotions. Celebrities, who are out and about incognito, often opt for enor-mous sunglasses, often drawing more atten-tion to themselves as a result—particularly if they are indoors in places where no one would normally wear dark glasses, e.g. hotel foyers, shoe stores, or at airport check-in desks.

Some people also resort to sunglasses after a particularly long night, which is why an inordinate number of people wear sunglasses on a Sunday morning at the bakery store—even when it is cloudy and overcast. This may well create a very casual look but it is cour-teous nonetheless to remove your sunglasses when in conver-sation with someone.

Classic pilots' sunglasses with slightly smaller lenses have been on the market for several years.

This thick-framed version is often combined with prescription lenses.

Bags for men

At one time, only mailmen wore shoulder bags but now a whole generation is doing so. In fact, in some parts of big cities nearly all the men seem to be carrying their stuff around in shoulder bags. Briefcases, on the other hand, seem to be a thing of the past.

However, this revolutionary development has not occurred just because men want to carry their laptops in a shoulder bag in order to leave both hands free—far more surprising is the fact that they now always seem to carry a "man bag" around with them. In the past, men only carried briefcases from home to work and back. Why was often a mystery, as the sandwiches, banana, and newspaper could easily have been stowed in a coat pocket. Presumably, a pigskin case symbolized that one was part of the working population. For this reason, unemployed people—in order to hide what was perceived as a shameful lack of a job—often left the house each day carrying a

Kreis, a firm manufacturing leather goods, also makes custom-made briefcases. The layout of the interior compartments is personally chosen by the client.

briefcase to preserve the illusion that they were off to work. Only a ridiculed minority used a man bag whilst the majority viewed the pockets in their clothes as adequate places to keep the things they might need during leisure hours, e.g. cigarettes, keys, and chewing gum.

Nowadays, a great many men (particularly those who are members of a generation which has been immortalized in literature) are following in women's footsteps and constantly carry a bag of stuff around with them—presumably digital communication gadgets, on the one hand, and other items of an obscure nature, on the other, e.g. bottles of mineral water, newspapers, scarves, or, what are now very large sunglasses' cases.

Coordination matters

THE ONLY REAL BAG FOR A MAN IS THE BRIEFCASE.

The first dilemma one faces when purchasing a briefcase is whether to buy black or brown? This is important for men who want their outfit to be coordinated down to the smallest detail. They know that a belt should be the same color as the shoes but does this also apply to a leather briefcase? As a general principle, the answer is yes, since a light-brown briefcase would be very conspicuous against black shoes. And vice versa—a black attaché case often looks very stark when combined with a light, summery outfit complete with beige suede shoes. Does it all come down to a choice between two types of briefcase, one brown and one black? Only if you actually do sometimes wear brown shoes to the office; if not, black remains the best option. Bolder souls sometimes opt for attaché cases in red, green, yellow, or even purple leather. This may seem eccentric but at least there would be no problem coordinating these colors since any of them would go with black as well as brown.

What a watch reveals

An Italian watch designer once commented that a man only needs three accessories: his car, his wife, and his watch. What is interesting here is that this man, whose livelihood is based on selling watches, does not mention the actual function of his products, which is to tell the time. Perhaps this is because even a cheap quartz watch can do this more accurately than the most expensive chronograph. There is no longer any correlation between the costly skills of a watchmaker and timekeeping reliability, which is why the business of marketing watches is now all to do with image. And the image is transferred to the wearer of the watch.

It is often asked whether you should turn up for an interview wearing an expensive watch, like a Rolex for example. There is no simple answer to this. For example, if a newly qualified law graduate is applying for a highly paid position in an established law firm, he is unlikely to go wrong wearing a discreet, stainless steel Rolex. It may be that his opposite number is also a watch enthusiast, who will immediately spot the timepiece and be favorably impressed by it. However, if the same applicant were applying for the job of in-house lawyer for a trades union-affiliated foundation, his Rolex timepiece may well be viewed disapprovingly. But that is only if

The Lange 1: flagship of this German firm.

The Richard Lange: pure excellence.

someone noticed it. Where watches are concerned, bear in mind Goethe's words: "One sees only what one knows." Only someone who knows about watches, who is therefore likely to be a watch fan himself, will recognize specific makes of watch. Anyone else would overlook such a detail—unless, of course, the watch was particularly conspicuous. Expensive watches are usually worn by affluent people and would, for the most part, only be noticed by others of their kind. In some countries, like Italy, however, it is relatively common for a man's accessories to include a luxury watch—even if this does not reflect the wearer's financial standing. Nowadays, it is not uncommon to see men in perfectly ordinary jobs, e.g. taxi drivers, barmen, or sales staff in a fashion store, wearing Swiss chronographs—in exactly the same way

that expensive cars are often seen in Germany parked outside modest homes. Anyone who does not have much money to spend but still wants a stylish watch should on no account resort to a fake Swiss watch, a cheap replica of the original. That would simply be tasteless. Better to buy a moderately priced watch, which can still hold its own in the style stakes. A classic in this respect would be a simple Swatch, a watch often worn by Italian men for fun, as an alternative to their Rolex, IWC, or TAG Heuer models. This type of watch would be a good option for the above-mentioned interview. It is stylish but modest—a combination that would never be frowned upon.

The Lange timepiece: distinctive.

The Datograph Perpetual: accurate until 2100.

Cuff links

Cuff links are accessories which have lost their original function and are now used predominantly for aesthetic reasons. They were originally invented in the late 19th century for use with starched cuffs. These were so stiff that it was impossible to fasten them with buttons. Modern shirt cuffs are usually so soft that they can be easily buttoned together. However, real fans of this type of jewelry, which always occurs in identical pairs, would consider this irrelevant. In their view, a shirt without any ornamentation on the cuff would be quite simply boring.

Cuff links are only obligatory with formal attire although they are also recommended for daytime wear with a dark suit. Even someone who prefers a more casual look can create additional interest with a pair of cuff links. There is, after all, nothing wrong at all with wearing them to accessorize a smart casual look as well, for example with chinos or corduroy pants and a sweater.

Hunting and shooting motifs are classic favorites for cuff links, as in this pair.

There are many different forms of stirrup-shaped cuff links, which fasten around the outside of the cuff.

The royal fleur-de-lys motif, combined with silver, lends a touch of elegance even to ordinary commoners.

Next to gold, gleaming sterling silver is still the most popular precious metal.

Yet many men would find that too fussy, or even overdressed. The rule of thumb is that cuff links are always appropriate with any outfit that includes a sports jacket or blazer. It does not necessarily have to include a necktie. Generally speaking, almost any identical pair of objects, which are small enough to fit through a button-hole, can be turned into cuff links. Small spheres or flat oval- or bean-shaped cuff links are very popular, as are cubes or tiny replicas of significant objects, such as golf balls, faucets (left "hot," right "cold"), cars, animals, or all kinds of tools. And anyone who inherits a pair of earrings, for example, can often have them reworked into cuff links. The most inexpensive type of cuff link is the tiny braided balls which can be purchased in a whole range of colors. These make a good substitute for more expensive cuff links and are ideal for picking up colors which appear elsewhere in the outfit. Anyone who likes wearing red socks, for example, could match these with a pair of red, braided, knot-type cuff links.

Colored, braided knots are more than mere substitutes for more expensive cuff links.

Scarves

A scarf is one of the oldest types of accessory. Human beings have been wearing scarves around the neck and head since they began working and weaving cloth. Men's fashion is no stranger to warm, woolen, or cashmere scarves for cold days, silk scarves to enhance an elegant coat, cravats to set off a shirt, jacket, pullover, or knitted cardigan, not to mention the many more decorative types of scarf in lighter fabrics which have been enjoying considerable popularity in recent years as a unisex accessory.

The fact that the scarf is often used as a substitute for a necktie is interesting from the perspective of fashion history, because the long modern necktie is descended from the cravat. For decades now the Italians have been a strong influence on trends. Pasta is part of our staple diet and we drink espresso or cappuccino instead of filter coffee, and prefer Latte Macchiato to "milky

coffee." Matters of fashion now provide a similar opportunity for us to express our Italian side. Sweaters are draped nonchalantly around the shoulders and scarves are no longer simply wrapped around the neck and knotted but instead are shaped into a decorative coil.

In the past, scarves were only worn as protection against the cold or sore throats. Nowadays, they are extremely popular all year round. It is true that scarves can be a very useful accessory even on warm days, for instance, to guard against drafts. On summer mornings or evenings, when it is still not quite warm but the temperature is nevertheless too high for a jacket or pullover, a scarf made of fine wool, cashmere, cotton, linen, silk, or any mixture of these fibers can be very useful.

Despite the close links between a scarf and a necktie, the dress code precludes them from being interchangeable. One cannot combine a cravat with a shirt under a business suit, at least not if you are aspiring to a classic business look. However, it is perfectly in order to wear a cravat with a sports jacket or suit for more formal leisure occasions, although too much experimentation gives rise to an impression of forced trendiness.

A scarf is one of the most important accessories—and not just in winter. Pictured here are some wool and cashmere scarves from the Dante collection.

SHINY SHOES AND IMMACULATE CLOTHES ARE MORE
IMPORTANT THAN EXPENSIVE BRANDS AND FANCY LOGOS.

Cleaning and care

Most people nowadays would never in a million years contemplate darning a hole in a sock. It would simply be thrown
away and replaced with a new one. Although this may be
good for retailers, this "throw-away" mentality is, if you think
about it, rather undesirable, since it almost inevitably implies
a reluctance to pay higher prices for more durable products.
There is a widely held notion nowadays that frequent purchases at bargain prices are somehow better than infrequent
purchases at what would be considered a normal price. After
adding up the cost, it may be that bargain hunters would
come out ahead but, even so, there are many reasons why
it is still better to pay a bit more for certain items.

Things were not always better in the old days—on the contrary, people looked after
their things, not because they worried about durability but because it was usually a
simple matter of necessity. Clothes were more expensive, had to last longer and were
cared for accordingly. Many men over the age of 40 will perhaps still remember the
concept of keeping a "pair of pants for best." These were made of wool and kept for
special occasions. This may sound old-fashioned but to some extent many people still
do this even now. They have suits in the wardrobe which are reserved for special occasions, just as some cars are only brought out of the garage on a Sunday. Nice things are
looked after—and cared for.

People who respect their things generally get to enjoy them for longer. But even
expensive products only last longer if they are treated properly. This does not cost much
and usually requires only minimal effort. It is regular attention that is crucial in this
respect and virtually all you need to do is adopt the habit of giving your suit a quick
brush and airing after each wear (ideally on a balcony or terrace, or, if necessary, by an
open window). Shoes do not have to be constantly polished to a brilliant shine, merely
treated with shoe cream or wax polish from time to time—in keeping with the motto:
a little and often.

*A night in the fresh air is the best treatment for a tired suit. Suits should be dry-cleaned as
little as possible.*

Basic rules for suit care

Speed is the key, so treat any marks as quickly as possible. Always work from the outside in toward the center in order to prevent rings or lines being left after the fabric has dried. Be sure to test the stain remover on the inside of the jacket first.

If household products do not work, you may have to resort to paying for chemical cleaning. Be careful, though, as many firms often do not treat the products with proper care and attention. Damaged or torn-off buttons are often the least of your worries in this respect. The consequences of unpro-

fessional pressing can be far worse. You are strongly advised, therefore, only to entrust your suit to a reliable specialist.

It is not only egg yolk and tomato ketchup that pose a threat to our clothes. Dust can also be very harmful to a good-quality suit. Millions of tiny particles can become embedded in the weave until it eventually becomes choked. For this reason, it is important to shake and brush the suit after each wear. Natural bristles offer the gentlest option for cleaning the fabric. Robust woolen materials respond well to

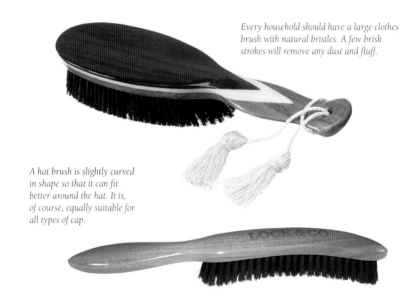

Every household should have a large clothes brush with natural bristles. A few brisk strokes will remove any dust and fluff.

A hat brush is slightly curved in shape so that it can fit better around the hat. It is, of course, equally suitable for all types of cap.

hog bristles, whereas a soft, goat's hair brush is kinder on more sensitive worsted fabrics or cashmere. After brushing, fold the pants flat along the crease and hang them up with the jacket on a broad, wooden clothes hanger. Thin, plastic hangers will eventually cause the shoulders of a jacket to lose their gently rounded shape.

If the fabric is badly creased, it will need steaming. This is done by running hot water into the bath until rising steam forms a thick mist in the bathroom. Hang up the suit for half an hour in the steamy atmosphere. This will remove the creases and give the fibers the chance to absorb moisture, which will restore their elasticity. A dose of damp, night air is also beneficial as well as the best way to get rid of stale tobacco odors. A hook on the wall of your balcony or terrace is therefore absolutely vital if you frequently consort with smokers. If your pants begin to lose their sharp crease, never press them with the iron directly on the fabric but always lay a damp, cotton cloth (light in color and well-washed) between the iron and the material. Otherwise ironing will make the pants shiny.

Dry, non-fatty dirt, such as sand, sawdust, dust, or crumbs, is easy to remove with a clothes brush. Mud should be left to dry first, otherwise the bristles will merely work it deeper into the weave.

Anyone who wants to avoid the continual worry of stains should steer clear of very light or delicate suit fabrics, which are extremely unforgiving when it comes to mud splashes or improper treatment of stains. Muted colors or patterned fabrics of more than 9 oz (300 gsm) can take more punishment.

(Above left) The cashmere brush is made with soft goat's hairs.
(Above) This small brush without a handle is designed for traveling.
(Left) The tweed clothes brush with its extra stiff bristles is good for removing dust from fabric.

ALCOHOLIC DRINKS, WINE
Blot up white wine or spirits with a dry cloth. Any lines that appear after the mark has dried may have to be sponged with hot, soapy water. If the wine stain has dried, it should first be treated with a mixture of alcohol and water and then blotted with white vinegar. Red wine stains should be sprinkled with a lot of salt, which should draw the liquid out of the fabric.

BALLPOINT PEN INK
Soak washable materials in cold water before washing them in the washing machine. If necessary, the stain may be further treated with 90 percent alcohol or concentrated bleach but only if the fabric in question is white or color-fast. Wool or silk can be treated with a solution consisting of one-third alcohol to two-thirds water.

BLOOD
Generally speaking, blood stains can be removed using cold water. If this does not work, cotton and color-fast fabrics can be treated successfully with a solution of diluted ammonia—but test first on an inconspicuous area of fabric. Delicate colors and wool can be treated with water containing soluble aspirin. Leave to work on the stain for a few minutes, then sponge with clear water.

CHOCOLATE
Wash in cold water. If this fails to remove the stain, try tackling it with 90 percent alcohol.

COFFEE AND TEA
Mix an equal quantity of alcohol and water and blot the stain with this solution. Then, sponge the stain with white vinegar. Caution: Do not use vinegar on linen.

EGG
Leave the egg to dry, then carefully scrape off any solid particles. Wash with laundry soap in cold water. If this fails to

stain removal

work and the fabric is white, the stain can be dabbed with hydrogen peroxide.

FAT, OIL In the case of cotton fabric, rub dry soap onto the stain and rinse in cold water. Dish liquid can also be drizzled onto the stain and left to work for a short while. Test the detergent first for color-fastness on an inconspicuous part of the fabric. Silk

can be dusted with talcum powder and then brushed clean.

GREASE, TAR These are extremely difficult to remove. Some experts recommend rubbing butter into the stain. Once this has dried, any solid particles can be scraped off with a knife and the remainder blotted with turpentine.

HOLES BURNED BY CIGARETTES OR CIGARS Burn holes have to be professionally repaired. Scorch marks on white cotton may be treated with diluted hydrogen peroxide; repeat the treatment using bleach before rinsing in warm water. Wool or silk fabrics should be treated by rubbing dry laundry soap into the mark. Leave for a while, then rinse out.

MAKE-UP AND LIPSTICK Blot cotton fabrics with 90 percent alcohol but use a good-quality stain remover on the more delicate fabrics.

NICOTINE Soak a cotton ball in 90 percent alcohol and carefully blot the stain.

WAX Use a spoon to remove as much of the wax as possible. Treat any residue with turpentine or benzene. Alternatively, place blotting paper or any similar absorbent material (paper towel or tissue etc.) over and beneath the stained area, then iron.

How to wash shirts correctly

To get the best results and end up with a perfectly laundered shirt, it is best to begin by sorting your laundry. There are two criteria in this respect: firstly, the recommended washing temperature and, secondly, the color. Anyone wishing to use a whitening detergent on white shirts should wash any colored shirts separately using a special color-safe detergent. As a precaution, dark-colored shirts should be washed individually while still new, or else with other items of a similar color. Anyone wishing to treat their laundry with extra care can place the items to be washed in a pillowcase or special washing bag. It is widely recommended that shirts should not be spun dry but hung on a washing-line while still dripping wet. Nor should shirts be dried in a dryer or they might shrink.

Regardless of whether they are spun or not, shirts should be ironed while still damp. In reality, however, it is difficult to put this advice into practice, since shirts almost always seem to reach their optimum level of dampness when you are too busy or with no inclination to do the ironing. A water spray or atomizer can be useful in this respect and the washing can be placed in a plastic bag to keep it uniformly damp. Or you can use a steam iron. The

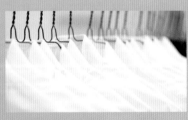

A small indulgence: having your shirts laundered.

A good-quality, mild detergent will protect your shirts.

Modern dryers offer a wide choice of programs.

latter does not produce as good a result as ironing a damp shirt but it is still reasonably effective. If a shirt is really badly creased, it can be ironed on both sides, first on the inside, then right side out. This trick also works with evening dress shirts with pleated fronts. If you have sufficient storage space, it is best to store your shirts on hangers or, if not, they should be carefully folded up.

Anyone who does not have time to look after his shirts can always send them to a laundry. If you find somewhere reliable, all you will have to do is drop off any shirts that need washing and they will be returned to you a short while later freshly laundered, either on hangers or lovingly wrapped in paper or cellophane. The high rate of competition in many big cities makes this service relatively affordable compared to rural areas, where it is generally too expensive. So-called non-iron shirts warrant a whole chapter to themselves. They are very popular but there are not many manufacturers who would guarantee crease-free shirts—and even then, only if the care instructions are followed to the letter. Non-iron shirts should be given no more than a short spin, or none at all, after which they should be hung and left to dry on a coat hanger. Some manufacturers recommend placing shirts in a moderately hot dryer, after which, if a shirt is still a bit creased, the advice is to put it on and let body heat do the rest. The specially treated fabric of which non-iron shirts are made leaves them rather less breathable than normal ones and may, in some cases, encourage odors. It is up to the individual to weigh up the advantages and disadvantages.

At the laundry, shirts are usually pressed by machine.

(Left) It usually costs extra to have shirts ironed by hand.

(Below) Perfectly pressed: collar and cuffs.

Brilliant result

Apparently, some stressed executives regard the task of cleaning their expensive shoes as an almost meditational relaxation exercise. What they invest in obligatory brushes, creams, and polishes is as much as an average man would spend on footwear over an entire year. Some men share this pleasure with other like-minded individuals, for example at the Club Swann in Paris. This club was founded in 1992 by clients of a high-class Parisian shoemaker. The inaugural meeting—by invitation only—

Reduced to a minimum but nevertheless very useful is this mini-set of creams, cloths, and brushes.

Smaller than the shoe case but still generously equipped: the maxi-set by Eduard Meier.

A luxurious leather case with all the equipment neatly to hand will make the task of shoe care an attractive prospect to any gentleman.

(Center) A turpentine wax polish, such as EM-2 by Eduard Meier, is a simple, basic, shoe-care item and invaluable for a wax-and-water polish.

Perhaps rather small for a birthday present but an excellent in-between gift. Ideal for traveling.

was held in the Hôtel de Crillon, a luxury hotel in Paris. Since then, intellectuals, artists, and entrepreneurs have met there once a year, to roll up their sleeves and polish their elegant *chaussures* to a brilliant shine while engaging in high-minded conversation—accompanied by champagne. Similar get-togethers are also held in Germany, e.g. at Eduard Meier's in Munich, Germany's oldest shoe manufacturer. The participants in these "shoe-polishing seminars" are all extremely sophisticated, and presumably generally well-to-do, but, in principle, the courses are open to everyone who is willing to pay the attendance fee. Even if you are simply not interested in such things, a basic amount of shoe maintenance is inescapable unless you simply do not care whether your shoes last a long time or are polished to a high shine.

Always use a shoehorn when putting on your shoes as this will protect the heel.

Buffing with a shoe bone on the flesh side of the leather can smooth out scratches, e.g. on horsehide or waxed calfskin.

(Center) Just like amateur chefs, shoe-care enthusiasts need aprons. They are very important in protecting clothes from nasty stains.

A mini shoe-bone in the form of a key ring is obviously more of a novelty than anything else but can still be put to good use.

A larger, buckhorn shoehorn will protect your shoes and spare your back.

The correct way

Preliminary cleaning
The first step is to remove any loose dirt or dust with a brush. Dried-on mud should be carefully scraped off using the back of a knife.

Leather milk
Shoes should not be washed too often. They can be cleaned instead with leather milk before the shoe polish is applied.

Shoe trees
Shoe trees should be inserted into the shoes after washing and also after every wear.

Application
Wax polish should be applied to the shoes using a soft brush. Do not use too much. Polish can still be applied even if shoes are wet from the rain or as a result of washing.

Drying
After their wax-and-water polish, shoes must be left to dry thoroughly to allow the resulting shine to harden.

Polishing
Ideally, your shoes should be given a final polish using a soft-bristle brush, which can, if so desired, be covered with a nylon stocking.

to clean shoes

Washing
If the shoes are still ingrained with dust or dirt after their preliminary clean, they can be washed. This is especially important for the soles in winter weather.

Washing
Washing will get the leather thoroughly clean—a soft brush will help in this respect. The same also applies to suede leather.

Applying shoe cream to the shoe soles
Remember to apply shoe cream to the bottom of the sole, especially the area under the arch. This makes it water-resistant and helps maintain its flexibility.

Polishing with wax and water
Dip the cloth in the wax, then add a little water and polish using a circular motion. Repeat this procedure several times until the shoe reaches the desired shine.

Suede leather shoe care
Suede leather shoes are easy to look after. Light dustings of dirt or dust can be removed simply by using a special brush.

Suede leather shoe care
New suede leather shoes should be generously sprayed with a waterproofing agent before wearing. Subsequent treatments will not need as much spraying.

How to care for your necktie

Just imagine if you knotted the legs of your suit pants several times a week. Even regular pressing would not prevent the fabric from soon being ruined. A silk necktie, on the other hand, manages to survive being tied into a Windsor or Four-in-Hand knot several times a week without difficulty, sometimes over a period of years. A minimal amount of care will extend its life even further.

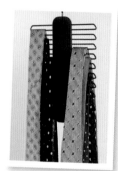

Very important: Undo the knot every time you take off your necktie. The gentlest way to do this is to loosen the knot, take the necktie off over your head and then undo it completely. Then wrap the necktie around your hand and leave it to rest, at least overnight. All creasing will usually have disappeared by the next day. If not, a few bursts of steam from an iron should do the trick. If you need to press a necktie, place a clean cotton or linen cloth over the fabric before ironing. Please do not iron sharp creases into a necktie; it needs to retain its soft, slightly tube-like character.

It is advisable to check occasionally that the tie's label is still firmly attached as it would be a pity if this were to be lost. It would also look rather untidy if it were hanging by a thread and poking out at the side. Jacquard silk neckties should occasionally be checked for damage around the edges at the broad end of the tie. It does not look good if the silk is starting to fray around the point.

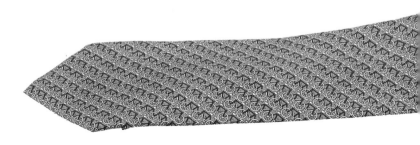

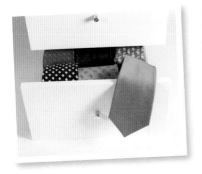

THE RIGHT WAY TO STORE NECKTIES

Anyone who only has one or two neckties has no need to worry too much about how to store them. If you are beginning to assemble a large collection, you should give some thought as to the best way of storing them.

As a basic principle, neckties can either be hung up or stored flat. The exception to this is knitted neckties, which prefer to be stored horizontally. The cheapest option is a clothes hanger, on which your neckties can be hung over the cross bar. Even three or four such hangers will not take up much space, although silky ties have a tendency to slip off the hanger. It is useful to separate them into a rough sort of order, e.g. one hanger for striped neckties, one

for ties with motifs on them, another for ones with geometrical designs, and so on. Alternatively, you can use special necktie hangers, which have a separate bar for each necktie. Care should be taken that none of these miniature hanging rails have any sharp projections which could snag the silk. The best way to store your neckties so you can view the full collection is to lay them in a drawer. They can either be folded in half (depending on the drawer size) or rolled up. The latter method not only allows you to see them all at a glance but also protects the neckties, as rolling them up makes creases disappear.

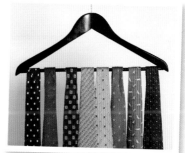

Glossary

A

Adjustable waistband Pants waistband which has a method of adjusting it inside the waistband. It replaces the pants belt. Adjustable waistbands are generally found on pants which are held up by suspenders (see also Stretch waistband).

Ascot An old-fashioned form of necktie, once worn with a morning coat or frock coat. Nowadays, would only be worn, if ever, with a wedding suit.

B

Batiste A lightweight, plain weave fabric made from very fine, high-grade yarns.

Beefroll American penny loafers, which get their name from the way the leather is sewn closed—reminiscent of a beef roll being tied.

Belt Strap, usually of leather, which is guided through loops around the waistband and designed to keep pants in position. The color of the belt should be coordinated with the shoe color.

Bemberg silk Brand name for a silk-like cotton lining used for suits, overcoats, and sports jackets.

Bespoke British term for custom tailoring. Originally used to mean that the fabric for the garment was "promised" to the client.

Blazer Dark blue double-breasted jacket with two side slits and gilt brass buttons, a style copied from the naval uniform. Can also signify a single-breasted, solid-color club jacket, usually with patch pockets and brass buttons. Occasionally striped to denote club colors.

Blucher A shoe with open lacing, also known as a Derby. The side parts of the shoe are stitched to the front section of the shoe. This part is also known as the vamp, and covers the instep and toes, extending into the tongue of the shoe.

Boat shoe A moccasin with leather shoelaces and a slip-proof, synthetic sole, developed for use on board a boat.

Bowler British term for a hard, felt hat with a rounded crown, known in the US as a derby. Originally created for William Coke by Lock's, the celebrated London hatmaker, it was designed as a protection for his gamekeepers' heads. Typical colors are black, gray, or brown.

Breeches Knee breeches or riding pants.

Brogue A type of Oxford shoe (see separate entry) with decorative perforations and wing tips. Also known as a Budapest because this style was also manufactured in Hungary. But the term "Budapest" is misleading, since the shoe was invented in Scotland.

Buffalo horn Material for buttons on top-quality suits and sports jackets. Lower-priced clothing will have buttons made from synthetic material.

Business casual A casual form of business attire, e.g. a combination of sports jacket and pants. Usually worn without a necktie. In many business sectors, this has now become more familiar than the dark suit.

Button-down shirt A shirt, the collar tips of which are buttoned to the shirt front. The original version of this is the button-down shirt with a "soft-roll collar" made by Brook Brothers in New York. The shirt can also be worn with a necktie and teamed with a business suit.

C

Caban Double-breasted, short coat, often in dark blue.

Cashmere Yarn or fabric made from the fine undercoat of the cashmere goat.

Cavalry twill Extremely durable and warm woolen fabric with a characteristic diagonal structure. Often used for pants, which are traditionally teamed with a sports jacket or blazer.

Chalk stripes Classic pattern for suit fabrics, consisting of white stripes on gray or blue, most common in double-breasted suits. They are so-called because the stripes look as if they have been drawn with chalk.

Chesterfield Business coat with concealed button panel, traditionally single-breasted in gray herringbone pattern with a black velvet collar. Also in blue, black, or beige.

Cheviot A hard-wearing, coarse, woolen fabric made from the wool of the Cheviot sheep. A fabric typically used for English sports suits and jackets.

Chinos Light-colored, cotton pants of military origin. Typical colors include khaki, beige, or light, coffee.

Cleaning This normally means the chemical cleaning (also termed "dry cleaning" of non-washable clothes with the aid of fat- and stain-removing chemicals. If this method is used too often, it will damage the garments as the cleaning process also removes natural oils from the fabric. Pressing also takes a considerable toll on the fabric. Brushing and airing your clothes are much kinder options.

Club necktie Originally a necktie sporting the colors of an English club and only issued to members. Nowadays, it is a general term for striped neckties.

Cordovan Another term for horsehide and a rare and expensive raw material for shoes. The part of the hide that can be used is the leather from the hindquarters of the horse, which only provide enough for just two round pieces of leather for two to three pairs of shoes. The American manufacturer Alden is considered the best producer of horsehide shoes.

Cotton The most important raw material in textiles, even ahead of virgin wool. In the 18th century, it supplanted linen as the predominant textile. Underwear, shirts, jeans, chinos, as well as gabardine raincoats are all garments typically made from cotton.

Cotton flannel Soft fabric in plain or twill weave, primarily used for leisure shirts.

Cotton twilll Hard-wearing, twill-weave fabric, mainly used for leisure shirts.

Covert coat No longer than knee-length, single-breasted overcoat of covert fabric, a medium-weight twill. Characterized by a concealed button panel, and by four simple, parallel lines of stitching at both the cuffs and the hem. It sometimes has a velvet collar.

Cravat A neckerchief or scarf, and a forerunner of the necktie. The word is derived from the word Hravat, meaning Croat in the Croat language—soldiers from Croatia used to wear a kind of cravat.

Cuff link A piece of jewelry and accessory used for fastening the cuff of a shirt sleeve. Usually worn with shirts and business suits. Obligatory with a tuxedo, morning dress, or tails.

Custom tailoring Garments are hand-made by a master tailor. The most traditional and most expensive way of producing a suit.

Cutaway front The angled front panels of a suit jacket or morning coat.

Cutter A custom tailor who constructs a pattern for his clients on the basis of their measurements, transfers it to the relevant fabric, and then cuts it out.

D

Denim Blue cotton fabric used for jeans. Name believed to derive from the French: Serge de Nîmes.

Derby A type of hard hat (see Bowler). Also used to describe a shoe with open lacing (see Blucher).

Dinner jacket The English term for what is known as a tuxedo in the USA and as a "Smoking" in some European countries.

Dogtooth check Casual, two-tone woven pattern for woolen fabrics. Popular for suits, sports jackets, and overcoats.

Donegal tweed Coarse, mixed, Irish tweed.

Double cuffs see Turn-back cuffs.

Double-breasted jacket Jacket with two panels of buttons and, generally speaking, six buttons. The top two buttons are a blind pair of buttons and only serve as decoration. Another type of double-breasted jacket has two pairs of buttons, in which case it is similarly, the lower pair which actually buttons up.

Duffel coat Short, single-breasted hooded coat with horn fastenings.

Dusty madder Traditional dyeing technique for silk, and also a term for certain necktie patterns. Typical of the distinctive dusty-looking finish, which mutes the otherwise rich colors. Dusty madder and heavy dusty madder silk neckties usually have paisley or foulard designs. The originals came from Great Britain.

E

End-on-end Shirt fabrics woven with two warp threads in different colors to create a characteristic multi-colored appearance (also known as fil-à-fil).

Evening dress or tails Black tails with a white bow tie are the most formal and festive type of evening dress. It is worn when the invitation specifies "white tie," cravate blanche, or "full evening dress." Evening dress consists of tails, a dress shirt with wing collar, stiff front panel and single cuffs, as well as a white vest of cotton piqué, top hat, and evening pumps.

F

Finishing The final processing stage after weaving, during which the fabric undergoes treatments such as washing and brushing. Finishing the fabric produces a sheen and a pleasant feel or "hand."

Fishtail pants Pants, which are designed specifically to be worn with suspenders. The rear portion is divided, forming two separate points. The most common type are waistband pants.

Fitting A custom tailor will try the partly finished garment on the client to check how well it fits. Three fittings are usual with a new client. Fittings are not usual with made-to-measure clothing, even though they are often technically possible.

Flannel Soft fabric, moderately heavy to heavy. The clinging quality of flannel is produced by the special way it is manufactured. The wool undergoes a fulling process until it becomes felted. Gray flannel is typically used as a suit fabric or for pants worn with a sports jacket.

Four-in-hand A simple yet most commonly used type of necktie knot. It is so-called after a club by the same name in 19th-century England.

G

Gabardine A twill weave fabric. Impregnated cotton gabardine is typically used for trench coats. Wool gabardine is a popular fabric for pants and suits.

Galon braid Silk braided stripe down the outside pants seam, copied from the silk trim on uniform pants. Tuxedo pants have a single silk stripe down the outside leg seam, whereas pants worn with tails have a double stripe.

Galoshes Rubber overshoes which protect shoes and feet from water or cold and help prevent slipping.

Gilet A kind of vest or waistcoat.

Gingham check A delicate shirt check, usually in light blue and white, or pink and white.

Glen plaid A colorful design, consisting mainly of blue or red check over a Glenurquhart check. This type of pattern was created for English landowners who settled in Scotland and had no clan plaid of their own. Their employees wore these artificially created checks, known as "district checks." The Glenurquhart check belonged to the estates of the Countess of Seafield. The hard-wearing pattern is ideal for "school, work, and travel." In England, it is a common design for casual suits, whereas in the US it is also accepted business wear.

H

Hacking jacket Another name for a riding jacket, from the verb "to hack" or ride. It is typically narrow-fitting and high-waisted, and has a long slit up the back and slanting pockets. The hacking jacket was the forerunner of the modern sports jacket.

Harris Tweed One of the best-known types of tweed. Only tweed woven in the Outer Hebrides in Scotland can carry this sought-after label. It comes in a large variety of strong colors and is ideal for hard-wearing sports jackets.

Herringbone Term used to describe a particular type of twill weave, in which the threads are interwoven diagonally. To create the distinctive herringbone effect, the direction of the thread is altered at certain intervals, producing a zigzag pattern. Herringbone can be light or heavy: Fine, gray herringbone is typical for business suits, and heavy herringbone tweeds are used for sports jackets and overcoats.

Homburg A hat with a stiff, slightly curved brim. Discovered by King Edward VII on a visit to the German spa resort of Bad Homburg. Next to the top hat, the Homburg is the most formal style of hat and is found in black, blue, gray, or brown.

Horsehair A type of interfacing made from linen fabric interwoven with horsehair. It is used for stiffening and shaping the lapels and chest panels of a suit jacket or sports jacket. Lightweight suits generally have minimal horsehair interfacing or none at all (see Interfacing).

House check Check pattern, exclusive to a particular brand (or fashion house) and used as a signature pattern, for example as a lining. The most famous "house check" is the distinctive Burberry check.

I

Interfacing, glued or fixed Layer of fabric inserted between the outer fabric and the lining of a sports jacket, intended to give shape across the chest. In the interests of speeding up the process, it is usually glued in place. It makes the outer fabric less flexible and can affect the way it hangs. Common in industrially manufactured jackets and suits.

Interfacing, loose Virtually invisibly stitched to the outer fabric behind the lapel, along the shoulder seam and breast pocket using a prick stitch. Typically used in tailor-made garments.

Interlining In traditional tailoring sewn into a suit jacket to give it shape. Merely glued in place in industrial production.

J

Jermyn Street A street in London near to Piccadilly Circus, where numerous, traditional shirtmakers are located. A symbol of quality and tradition for the classic English shirt, which, in comparison to its Italian counterpart, is usually more strongly colored and more generously cut.

K

Kent collar Turn-down collar, the points of which are relatively close together. The standard collar to wear with a suit.

L

Last Simplified model of a human foot. In ready-to-wear footwear, the last is made to a standard size while custom-made shoes are made from a last shaped according to the actual client's measurements. The custom shoemaker's hand-made last is carved from wood and the shoe is fashioned around it.

Lining A cotton, silk, or viscose layer of material on the inside of a garment. The lining conceals any interfacing in the jacket, prevents the jacket becoming soiled by perspiration, and allows the garment to slide smoothly and elegantly over the other garments. A half-lined summer jacket, generally speaking, is also lined around the shoulders to make sure that it sits correctly. Pants are usually lined as far as the knee or, in the case of particularly coarse fabrics, down to calf level. The lining in durable made-to-measure suits can be replaced if it becomes worn after many years of wear.

Loden A fulled then brushed woolen fabric which is relatively waterproof and wind-resistant. It is used in traditional Austrian and German costume and also in hunting attire. The green loden overcoat is popular throughout the world as well as in its native countries.

M

Macintosh English term for a raincoat made of rubberized cotton, also known as "mac" for short. No longer considered fashionable, now that modern, purpose-made materials are lighter and more efficient.

Made-to-measure clothing The modern alternative to the traditional custom suit made by a tailor. The division of labor and the fact that they are largely industrially manufactured allows these clothes to be produced more quickly and more cheaply. To ensure the garment fits better than a ready-to-wear version, a standard pattern size is adapted to the individual client's measurements. Traditional bespoke tailoring is considerably more expensive but the garment is hand-made and will usually be a better fit.

Madras check A check that originated in India and is used for lightweight cotton fabrics, popular for leisure shirts, sports jackets, and golf pants.

Mako Type of Egyptian cotton which produces high-quality yarn, e.g. for batiste.

Marcella Textured woven fabric used for the shirt fronts, collar, and cuffs of traditional evening dress shirts.

Merino wool The heavily crimped wool of a merino sheep is the finest wool in the world and most suit fabrics are made from this. Australia is the main supplier.

Moccasin Term for a shoe made from one piece of leather which is drawn up and around the last, therefore functioning both as the outer sole and as the upper of the shoe. A boat shoe is a typical type of moccasin.

Mohair An extremely crease-resistant fabric with a slight sheen, mohair is made from the wool of the Angora sheep. Ideal for tuxedos and summer suits.

Moleskin Soft, warm cotton fabric in atlas weave—a popular fabric for casual pants, sports jackets, suits, and overcoats. Moleskin pants are often available in very strong colors.

Monkstrap Shoe which fastens with a buckle rather than laces.

Morning dress Tailcoat with rounded cutaway, also commonly known as a "swallow tailcoat." Worn for formal occasions during the daytime.

N

Necktie The most important element of formal dress, alongside the suit, shirt, and shoes, and a symbol of business attire throughout the Western world.

Norfolk jacket A tweed jacket with three or four buttons, a belt or half-belt at the back, box pleats and roomy pouch pockets for holding bullets and provisions. Regarded as the forerunner of the sports jacket. First worn in the 19th century on the country estates of the Duke of Norfolk.

O

Ostrich leather Made from ostrich hide with its very distinctive structure. Frequently used in the manufacture of small leather goods, for example, briefcases and wristwatch straps, but also used to make shoes.

Overdressed Being too formally or festively dressed. More embarrassing at private occasions than elsewhere.

Oxford fabric A type of weave, whereby dyed and undyed cotton threads are interwoven to produce a soft but very hardwearing shirt fabric. Oxford fabrics also appear a little less delicate and more formal than batiste or poplin.

Shoes: The most formal style of men's shoe with closed lacing and an undecorated toecap. Black Oxfords are the classic shoes to wear with a pinstripe suit, or with morning dress for a state reception, wedding, or funeral. Brown Oxfords can be worn with casual suits.

P

Paisley An Oriental design, symbolizing fertility. Mainly found on scarves, neckties, and dressing gowns.

Pea coat Short, double-breasted naval-style coat in dark blue (see Caban).

Peccary Natural, top-grained leather made from the hide of wild pigs, traditionally used for gloves.

Penny loafer Casual slip-on shoe from, originally worn during leisure hours or by students. The name comes from the custom of slotting a coin under the crosspiece as a talisman.

Pin stripe Wool fabric with a pattern of very thin, white stripes, which look as if they are made from a line of innumerable tiny pin pricks. White pin stripes on a blue fabric are typical for business wear.

Pinpoint This fabric is similar to Oxford fabric but rather finer, with a weft and warp in different colors.

Plaid Originally a woolen overweave in clan colors, part of Scottish national dress. The English term encompasses any kind of Scottish plaid and the patterns are also often used for blankets—particularly for travel blankets.

Pleats Pleats incorporated below the waistband give greater fullness to the pants at the front and disguise the pocket contents. The classic design will have two pleats on either side, one of which extends into the front crease, and a further pleat between this and the side pocket.

Plus fours Voluminous type of knickerbockers—or knee breeches. So-called because an additional "four inches" were added to the knee length in order to allow for the required overhang.

Pochette Pocket handkerchief.

Polo shirt Short-sleeved leisure shirt of cotton piqué with a soft collar and gathered sleeve cuffs. Classic component of casual and smart-casual wear.

Poplin Shirt fabric in plain weave with considerably more warp than weft threads. Available as single- or two-ply poplin depending on the threads used.

Prince Albert knot A necktie knot which is tied in much the same way as the four-in-hand except that the broad end is wrapped around the narrow end several times before the knot is complete. The result is a relatively thick but longish knot.

Pumps Flat men's pumps, often with a black bow of corded silk (grosgrain), are traditionally worn with evening dress and sometimes with a tuxedo.

Pajamas Night attire with wide pants, the name derives from the Persian term "pay jamah" meaning foot or leg garment. Usually made from cotton fabrics. Summer styles may have short sleeves and legs.

R

Raglan sleeve Sleeve cut in such a way that it forms part of the shoulder and extends up to the collar, named after Lord Raglan. Raglan sleeves are traditionally found on raincoats. They can either be cut as a single piece or consist of two pieces. The one-piece sleeve lies flatter on the shoulder. The more common type of sleeve is the set-in sleeve.

Ready-to-wear clothing Clothes which are not made to a client's individual measurements but for an imaginary standard figure. The advantage of ready-to-wear is instant availability in a wide price range; the disadvantage lies in the imprecise fit.

Regimental necktie Necktie in the colors of an English regiment, worn with civilian dress. Nowadays, usually used to describe any striped tie (see Club necktie).

Roman stripes Broad stripes on suit shirts, e.g. dark-blue stripes on white.

S

Saddle shoe Traditional American shoe with closed lacing, in which the side pieces form a saddle shape across the middle of the foot. The saddle is usually a different color from the rest of the upper. Also often worn as golf shoes.

Savile Row Street in London's Mayfair district, in which the most celebrated men's tailors in the world are located. Synonymous with the English gentleman's suit. Spiraling property rents have driven many tailoring establishments out of Savile Row in recent years, making way for a growing number of international designer labels.

School tie A necktie designed in the colors of a particular school or university, worn by its pupils and students, both past and present. See also Club necktie and Regimental necktie.

Sea Island cotton This usually refers to the most expensive quality of cotton shirt fabrics. Woven from a larger number of threads than poplin, which gives this fabric a silky feel. The finest men's socks are also made from Sea Island cotton.

Shepherd's plaid Small, check pattern, usually in black and white. Typically found as a suit fabric.

Shetland wool Wool from the Shetland Islands off Scotland, popularly used to make rustic sweaters, often in cable pattern. Also for mixed woven fabrics of carded wool, used for casual suits, sports jackets, and overcoats.

Shoe tree A block of wood shaped in the form of a foot, which fills and stretches the inside of the shoe when it is not being worn. Helps to keep the shape of the leather and also absorbs moisture. Many experts regard using a shoe tree as part of general shoe maintenance.

Shrink-resistant This means that a fabric will only be susceptible to a minimal degree of shrinkage. Good weaving mills are able to guarantee a shrinkage rate of no more than 1.5 percent.

Silk Traditionally a high-quality material for neckties, shirts, suits, and pajamas, but also used as lining and as a yarn in men's tailoring. Made from the cocoons of certain silkworm moth varieties, for example the larvae of the mulberry silkworm moth. Usually bred in captivity, as the production of silk from wild silkworms is relatively negligible. Can be woven into various types of weave.

Single-breasted suit Jacket with a single button panel and two or three buttons. In the case of a two-button jacket, only the top button is fastened, with a three-button one, the middle one is fastened—or the upper two, or all three.

Slip-on Coat with raglan sleeves, concealed button panel, and small lapels. The raincoat version is most usually made from cotton gabardine.

Slits Side slits or a central slit prevent the panels or back of a jacket from riding up when the wearer is seated. They were originally devised for riding outfits. From the 1930s to the 1950s, jackets without slits were the norm for business attire or evening dress.

Smart-casual Elegant, leisure look. Smartly casual. (see Business casual).

Sporting suit or jacket This rather old-fashioned term denotes a suit made from fabrics with patterns which suggest a more countrified style, e.g. checks, herringbone, or dogtooth check. Formerly worn in leisure hours or for traveling. The antithesis of this would be the dark-colored business suit. Nowadays, acceptable as business casual or smart casual.

Sports jacket Single-breasted jacket, which is not part of a suit, nor is it a blazer. This type of jacket became popular during the 19th century and imitated the English riding jacket and the Norfolk jacket. With its rounded lines and somewhat shapeless silhouette in comparison to the tailcoat, people of the period regarded it as rather sack-like. Often made of tweed, the urban version can be made from cashmere and other woolen fabrics, usually check. It should not be confused with the blazer (see that entry).

Spread or cutaway collar Shirt collar with collar tips which are set wide apart. After the Kent (or spread) collar (see that entry), this is the second most popular type of classic collar.

Stretch waistband Elastic pants waistband. The width of the waistband is adjustable by buckles. Also available in pants worn with suspenders.

Suit A jacket, pants, and vest of the same material. After World War I, the suit became accepted business attire for the office and special occasions. The basic shape of the suit has scarcely changed since that time.

Super 100 Lightweight, crease-resistant and shape-retaining new wool fabric used for summer clothing.

Suspenders Traditional suspenders are buttoned to the waistband while modern versions are fastened with clips. Typical of the English gentleman look.

T

Tartan Diverse types of check, which identify the various Scottish clans. Now, a generic term for all types of Scottish plaid patterns. We find tartan throughout the wardrobe, typically as a lining, for neckties, vests, and pants.

Tassel loafer Loafer, in which the laces are fed through eyelets or "tunneled" all around the shoe and then tied into a bow across the instep. The ends of the laces are decorated with little leather pompoms, also known as "tassels."

Tattersall check Check shirt for casual wear with the distinctive check of dark brown, green, wine red, blue, or black stripes on a white or beige background. The name

was inspired by the horse market owned by Richard Tattersall, where this check pattern was a traditional one for the horse blankets. The design is also used for vests, linings, and blankets.

Ticket pocket Small, additional pocket just above the right jacket pocket. Usually found on sports jackets and commonly used as a coin pocket.

Tie Another word for necktie or bow tie.

Top hat The most formal hat of all, only worn for daytime events as an accessory to morning dress, or for evenings, to round off evening dress or tails. There is also the collapsible top hat, or chapeau claque, which can be collapsed down for easy transport or storage.

Trench coat A belted, double-breasted coat of water-resistant cotton gabardine. First worn by British troops during the Boer War 1895–1902. The epaulettes and D-shaped metal rings on the belt, which were originally used to attach various pieces of equipment, are reminiscent of the trench coat's military past. Often fitted with a detachable wool lining for winter.

Trilby A narrow-brimmed felt hat possessing a thin hat band. It was originally part of the classic gentleman's look (especially in brown), but now fashionable in various styles and colors.

Trouser cuffs A relatively recent innovation, dating from the second half of the 19th century. Originally, the hems of pants were rolled up in order to stop them getting dirty or wet. Nowadays, a cuff is a common way of finishing off the trouser hem. Cuffs are uncommon in formal pants (i.e. with morning dress, tuxedo, or tails). Also found as turned-up cuffs on sleeves.

Turn-back cuffs Traditional cuffs on a man's shirt are fastened using cuff links. They give a perfect, clean finish to the sleeve, especially with shirts worn with a suit or sports jacket. Also known as double cuffs.

Tuxedo Often known as "tux," for short, a men's semi-formal jacket named after the Tuxedo Country Club in New York State. Known as a "dinner jacket" in England and a "Smoking" elsewhere in Europe. Can traditionally also be worn during the daytime for weddings.

Tweed Warm, heavy-wearing woolen fabric made in the British Isles, usually Scotland, which consists of several different colors of wool fibers woven together. The name supposedly derives from "tweel," the Scottish word for twill. Popular for sports jackets, suits, overcoats, and caps.

Twill A twill-weave fabric, easily identifiable by its parallel, diagonal lines. Strong, and heavy-wearing, it is a popular fabric for casual shirts.

U

Ulster Long men's coat with a half-belt at the back.

Underdressed To be not dressed formally or festively enough. A serious faux-pas, particularly in business circles.

V

Vest Part of a gentleman's outfit since the 17th century, was also originally an integral part of the suit, which developed during the late 19th century. The vest has not been an essential part of a suit since the Second World War (see Gilet).

Vicuña Very valuable hair from a South American camelid, resembling a llama. Gathering the hair is very labor-intensive and unrewarding. Small amounts of hair snagged on bushes or scrub are gathered by hand. For many people, a vicuña suit or coat is the epitome of luxury.

Vintage The fashionable name for second-hand clothing and accessories.

Viyella Warm shirt fabric, invented in 1890 by Henry Ernest Hollins. It consists of 55 percent merino wool as well as 45 percent long-staple cotton.

Voile Extremely thin and transparently sheer, this fabric may be used for dress shirts or light and airy summer shirts.

W

Warp and weft A fabric is produced by interweaving threads lengthwise and crosswise (see Weave). The lateral threads, which are carried over and then under the longitudinal warp threads, are known as the weft.

Wax-and-water polish A traditional shoe-polishing method, whereby an application of turpentine wax polish is then polished to a shine using a damp cloth. Since grease and water do not mix, the damp cloth does not wipe off the wax polish during this procedure but polishes the shoe to a high shine.

Weave The rhythm in which the warp and weft are woven together. There are three basic weaves: plain weave, twill weave, and atlas weave.

Whipcord A mixed wool fabric used for heavy-duty sports suits or pants worn with a sports jacket.

Windsor knot This was allegedly, the neck-tie knot favored by the Duke of Windsor, but experts can always be found to claim that the abdicated king actually preferred a four-in-hand knot, which derived its volume from a thick layer of interfacing within the necktie. The Windsor knot is the best option for shirts with a "cutaway collar," however, the narrower and slightly asymmetrical four-in-hand tends to look better as a rule. The half Windsor knot is slightly less voluminous.

Wing tips The curving wings of a man's shoe are called "wingtips." A shoe with a wingtip is known as a brogue or Budapest (see the relevant entry).

Y

Yarn Yarn is produced by twisting strands of fibers together. The yarn is called two- or four-ply, depending on how many fibers are involved. Having more fibers gives the yarn more strength and it also becomes more crease-resistant once the fibers are twisted together.

Index

Picture credits

The vast majority of images, which are not mentioned below, are new additions by photographer Erill Fritz (erill.fritz.fotografien.).

c=center, r=right, l=left, a=above, b=below

© adidas AG, Herzogenaurach: 110, 111 l., 160, 161
© Aida Barni, Prato: 190 b.r.
© Alan Paine, Nottinghamshire: 108, 109 a.l., a.r., b.l.
© Alden Shoe Company, Middleborough: 150 c.
© Alumo AG, Appenzell: 24
© Ascot Karl Moese GmbH, Krefeld: 38, 46, 47, 184
© Belvest, Piazzola sul Brenta: 12, 80, 136, 137, 188
© Bernhard Roetzel, Berlin: 17 a., 18, 19, 22, 25, 32, 33, 129, 142, 143, 171, 182, 183, 189, 207
© Chelsea Farmer's Club, Berlin: 71
© Converse Inc.: p. 158/159 b., 159 a.
© Cove & Co., Düsseldorf: 50-53, 56-57, 60-63, 68-70, 72, 73, 75 a., 76/77, 79, 172, 173
© Crockett & Jones, Northampton: 150 a.r.
© Edsor Kronen, Berlin: 39, 64
© Eduard Meier, Munich: 149 c., b., 166, 167, 169, 185, 214-217
© Emanuel Berg (Shirtmakers Family GmbH), Rösrath: 16, 28, 29, 65
© Eton, Gånghester: 26, 27 b.l., b.r., 34 a., b.l., 35 a., b.l.
© G B Kent & Sons Ltd., Hemel Hempstead: 20 c., 208, 209
© Gucci Group, Amsterdam: 20 a.r., b.l., b.r., 144

© Jörg Rausch, www.leder-info.de: 155
© KREIS Ledermanufaktur, Bernd Kreis, Obertshausen: 190, 191, 198, 199
© Lange Uhren GmbH, Glashütte: 200, 201
© picture-alliance: 14 c.
© picture-alliance/Bildagentur-online/ Sunny Celeste: 8/9
© picture-alliance/dpa: 9, 14 a., c., 15 a., b., 140 r., 141 l.
© picture-alliance/dpa/dpaweb: 15 (3rd fr.a.)
© picture-alliance/Eventpress hr: 141 r.
© picture-alliance/jazzarchiv: 140 l.
© picture-alliance/ZUMA Press: 15 (2nd fr.a.)
© Red Wing Shoe Company, Red Wing: 162, 163
© Robert Bosch Hausgeräte GmbH, Gerlingen-Schillerhöhe: 212 r.
© Roensberg Manufaktur, Berlin: 202 a.l., b.
© Scabal SA, Brussels: 23, 31, 112-115, 170, 174, 175
© Superga, Turin: 158 a.
© The Timberland World Trading GmbH, Munich: 82, 83, 88-95, 98, 99 b., 100, 101, 106, 107, 111 r., 151, 164, 165
© Tony Lama: 154
© Unilever Deutschland GmbH, Hamburg: 212 b.l.
© Windsor, Strellson AG, Kreuzlingen: 10, 11
© Zegna, Trivero: 176-181